Joe Kwon's
True Ghost Stories

Real-Life Encounters!

Volume 1

Ghost Stories from Around the World!

More Than 100 Recent Encounters From Over 45 Countries!

© 2010 Joe Kwon, Inc
All Rights Reserved

I

Joe Kwon's True Ghost Stories

VOLUME 1

Ghost Stories from

Around the World

Joe Kwon, Inc.

Joe Kwon's True Ghost Stories. Copyright 2010 by Joe Kwon, Inc. All rights reserved. Published and distributed worldwide from the United States of America. No part of this book may be used or reproduced in any manner whatsoever without written permission except in the case of brief quotations embodied in critical articles or reviews. For information, address Joe Kwon, Inc, 3 North Lafayette, Marshall, Missouri 65340.

ISBN-10 0-9828659-7-X

ISBN-13 9780982865972

Compiled by

Joe Kwon, Inc

Edited by Tom Kong

Special Thanks to

Tom Bolling and his Brother Joe

Also, a thanks to all those throughout the world who have shared their own encounters with us to make this compilation a reality, whereby the rest of us may consider ourselves warned that spirits do exist, and not all of them are friendly

Table of Contents

Just Wanna Say Hello 1
The Bride 2
The House With the Vortex 4
My Grandfather 6
Bright Eyes 8
The Bird 9
Black Out 10
Take Care of My Children 11
The Little Boys 14
Stalking Headless Ghost Soldier 16
My Older Sister's Daughter 18
The Black Shadow 20
Silent Stranger 20
Slapping Poltergeist 23
Ghost Bruises in Sweden 25
My Son Came to Say Goodbye! 26
Woman in White 28
The Lost Tiki 29
Dia de los Muertos (Day of the Dead) 33
The Old Man vs. The Boy 35
Baby Boy Aged 2 37

v

Hello? Who is Calling?..38
Unexplainable 39
Ghostly Strength 40
Ghost in the Backyard..42
Frightening Wake Up 43
Spirit Confused By Instant Death.....................................44
Risen...45
Journey Out Of My Body..46
Respiratory Therapist..47
Business Trip Nightmare..49
Sail Away..51
A Mexican Haunting 53
Colonial Ghost 55
My Cousin's Special Gift..58
Business Trip Encounter 60
Jay's Grave 63
The Hand in the Bath 65
The Other Side..66
DEATH...68
The Shadow People 70
The Evil Girl...75
Disturbing The Jinns 76
Great Uncle George Comes to Play..................................79

VI

The Dirt Road	80
Death	82
Demon Chasing Me in the Cemetery	84
Someone in the Room	86
Blackness	87
Pig	89
Knock Knock Knock . . .	91
Meeting the Man with No Face	96
The Mysterious Giggles	98
She Scared Me But I Forgave Her	101
The Lakes	103
Mountain Man	104
The Wee Laddie	105
Man with a Lantern	107
Imaginary Friend	108
Hard Worker	110
Third Day	115
Strange Child	115
The New Car	117
The Dead Bat Lady	118
Perverted Ghost	121
The Ghost of a Student	122
Demon Child	124

Haunted Church?	127
A Ghostly Comrade	132
The House On Attawandaron Road	135
Footprints	137
The Cemetery Demon	140
In Good Hands	141
The Closet Mirror	142
Working In The Plantation	144
Singing Lady	146
Disturbing a Spirit in Thailand	147
Marked By a Dream	150
The Lonely House	151
Highway Spirit	153
Jinn Encounter in the Woods	153
Poltergeist	158
Santa Maria Del Mexicano (Boarding School)	161
The Black Shadow	163
The Demon Head	164
The Locket	166
The Clone	168
Ready or Not Here I Come	169
Grandmother	170
The Souls of Dead Babies	172

Demon Dad	175
Poltergeist In The House	177
The Pale Man	178
No Eyes!	180
No Face!	181
Is She Dead? Am I Crazy?	182
I Love You Darling	184
Nightmarish Nights	187
The Rose	192
Tom	195
The Lady In White	197
My First Ghost	199
My Grandmother's House	200

x

XI

Just Wanna Say Hello
Tonga

This is a true story that happened to my sister while she was visiting her husband's family in Tonga. She had a few paranormal things happen to her while she was there and used to tell me these stories as a child.

It was the year '93 or '94, and my sister who I will name Sarah, had had her first child with her husband and went to see his family in Tonga. I'll name him Tom. Tom's grandmother was still alive, but his grandfather had passed before he could meet his great granddaughter.

One night Tom had taken himself and his new baby to bed early, while my sister stayed up with some of his family members playing cards. The bedroom he was sleeping in was the very next room over. After a few hours of playing, my sister heard Tom calling out her name and telling her to come, in Tongan. She went to the room and walked in and froze. Standing next to the bed beside her husband and her baby was a ghostly man. He wasn't solid, but she could clearly see that he was male and of the same origin as her husband. He was just standing there touching her baby on the forehead.

She said to Tom to move, get the baby and get up. But he replied he was frozen and couldn't move a muscle. Tom is a very dark skinned man. He was so afraid, he had literally turned as white as the sheet he was lying on. Sarah just fell to her knees and started praying, asking God to protect her and her family. When she looked up again he was gone and Tom was able to move again.

Sarah asked Tom if he knew who the man was and he replied it was his grandfather. He had come to say hello to the new baby. The next day Tom's grandmother and some other elders went to the cemetery where he was buried to do some sort of ritual to his grave. This was meant to ensure the baby's safety and to ensure that his spirit stayed where it was suppose to.

This was one of the few experiences she had while visiting Tonga.

The Bride
India

My experience takes place in India. I was 12 years old and was visiting with my family. We went often and I had made a few friends. I had my own room there and the house was pretty creepy so I begged my friend Ruby to stay with me for the first few days. Her mom said it was fine.

During the day we went exploring all around the village and the countryside. We were told by Ruby's older sister we couldn't go out to play around the ditch area... there wasn't any water in there just an empty ditch with trash and junk in it. She made it clear that between 12pm-2pm, she said it was the time the dead walk. We were to be indoors!

Volume 1 Ghost Stories from Around the World

We were confused, but more curious. So, of course, we had to sneak out and go straight to the ditch, which was about 15 minutes outside the village. We just found a bunch of candles that someone had been lighting. On our way back we ran into this older lady mumbling something and sounded like she was crying. Ruby knew who she was and told me to keep walking. I didn't think much of it and we were soon home.

That night we watched a movie and went sleep around 1:30am. I woke up in the middle of the night really hot and sweaty. I opened the windows and got back into bed. I went back to sleep and woke up again a few minutes later really hot. Looked at Ruby and she was sleeping. I noticed that there was someone sitting on the table at the foot of my bed. The moonlight was coming in and I could see it was a woman wearing a red dress. (Indian brides usually wear a shade of red.) I could see her big eyes wide open and she wasn't blinking. Her face looked swollen. I could see her jewelry glittering and her make-up. I could see she had tears on her cheeks that weren't moving. I was so scared at that point... I went under the covers and started praying.

Every time I peeked out she was still there. I was too scared to wake Ruby up or even move. I finally fell back to sleep and woke up around 9am. Ruby was already up and in the kitchen helping my mom. I ran out of the room to tell my mom what happened. As I was telling my mom my aunt had walked in. Ruby just listened silently not surprised at all. My aunt started yelling at Ruby, telling ruby she should have known better. My mom and I were confused.

My aunt then told us. There was a young girl who had just

passed away a few months ago. She had an arranged marriage because the guy she had been seeing was really poor and her dad was completely against the relationship. So she was forced to marry this stranger her dad chose. The day after her forced wedding she came back to her parent's house and made it clear she was not gonna stay with this man she was forced to marry. She had arranged to run away with her boyfriend.

As soon as her dad figured this out he choked her to death. Made it look like she had been accidently electrocuted. Paid the cops off of course, and there was no investigation, but the whole village knew what happened.

She was haunting the house she was killed in. All of the neighbors have claimed to see her ghost. Her mother had been trying different prayers and had thrown her belongings into the ditch to try and get rid of her. That was the lady we had seen mumbling. My aunt said the ghost must have followed us back home. She just wanted justice. Her murderer was free. We had the house blessed right away, and had no problems the rest of our vacation. We still weren't allowed out of the house 12pm-2pm or 12am-2am.

The House With the Vortex
Auckland, New Zealand

My family and I moved to New Zealand when I was 4. The first few years in the house were uneventful for my sister, dad and myself, but my mum was seeing floating mists and going through cold spots on the stairs.

Volume 1 Ghost Stories from Around the World

When I hit puberty (which is when ghosts usually go into a frenzy) things started happening in quick succession. My fire alarm would go off repeatedly at night. Thinking it was faulty my mum and dad replaced the batteries and pulled it apart but it still happened.

While doing my homework one day, my hair was flicked. Thinking it was my sister I quickly turned around to yell at her but there was no one. With my heart about to rupture out of my chest in fear I shakily said, "Ha-ha very funny," and walked out of the room.

My other family members were starting to see, hear and smell things. My dad was engulfed in cigar smoke most nights while my sister was woken up by her bed shaking and on a separate occasion seeing a women standing next to her desk playing with her pens.

Probably the most frightening thing that happened to me was when I was made to sleep in the rumpus room next to my sister's room. Now before I go on, my parents had people come over that deal with contacting spirits, and they said we had a vortex (a portal between their world and ours) in between the rumpus room and my sister's bedroom. So, no matter how many times the house got cleared of spirits, more would come back. I was just about to fall asleep when I saw a woman in white floating in my sister's doorway with her mouth open in a silent scream. Totally freaked out (I was only 10), I put my head under the covers and told myself to be brave. I eventually poked my head out only to see a man in the study doorway in full World War 1 or 2 uniform, on a crutch as he was missing a leg. I don't know how I did it but I did fall asleep after that.

Other things happened in the 8 years we were there but none as significant as these. I'm 23 now and living in Australia. I still get freaked out when remembering these occurrences. but I think my sister is worse off. She is younger so I think it affected her more. She's 21 and up until about 2 years ago (because her boyfriend moved in) she still slept with a nightlight on and she NEVER speaks of what happened.

She still lives with my parents and she doesn't know that they have a resident spirit living with them as well. If she ever found out she would be out of there with no hesitation.

My Grandfather
Gurabo, Puerto Rico

I never knew who was my paternal grandfather. What I know is that my father grew up in Spain. When he was 14 years old, he moved to Puerto Rico with his mother and stepfather.

The years went by, he met my mother and got married. I have an older brother.

Everybody in the family says that I have a strong personality from an early age. When I got mad I just stood there and stared at the person and said nothing, just stared. Now I think about it and it is kind of creepy.

In my college years I had a boyfriend. I remember it was a difficult relationship, because I had to do things his way. I also worked in this bookstore. It is here where I started wondering more about my grandfather. My father always told me that he died when he was small and that he didn't remember seeing him, spending time with him. I asked for pictures. Nothing. Nada. Just another mystery.

One day this man walked in the store. He was dressed all in white. He is what we call in the Islands a "santero." He looked at me And said, "Here, he wants you to have this." And handed me a hand-size pink candle. I said, "Excuse me Sir, but who wants to give me this?" He answered, "Your grandfather, the Gypsy."

Honestly, I felt he was joking. I was going to reply by thanking him and ignore everything, but then he told me that I should believe him, that my grandfather is with me always, and that he gets very angry toward people that treat me in a wrong way. He even gave me a description of him. Very similar to my father, except in height. He told me that he is a tall man. My father is not that tall. Now I knew it was not a joke.

That same day, my boss called to my attention in front of everyone. She didn't know I was on my break and asked what I was doing standing there doing nothing. I told her I was on my break and right in front of me on top of a table was her bottled water. I moved it and laid my hand for a few seconds touching it. The next day she called in sick because she caught the flu. I swear I did not wish any bad thing to happen to her. That day, the same man walked in and said, "I told you he gets mad at people that treat you unfair." Ok now I confessed that I was starting to believe about the Gypsy grandpa.

That same week, my then boyfriend was arguing about some insignificant issue and I was getting a little anxious. He parked his car in front of my parents' house and continued fighting with me. Suddenly, he closed his mouth, his eyes wide opened, pale. He looked like he was going to cry. He was starting to drive again when I asked him what happened? I told him that he looked like he just saw a ghost. He told me that he saw the face of a man next to me staring at him very angrily. I stared looking at him in shock. I said, "You should take me back to my house right now."

I am 34 years old and still don't know the name of my grandfather. Still don't know for sure if he was a Gypsy. It is still a mystery in the family. What I know is that from that day on I can tell you that whoever he is, I feel his love for me and he still watches over me...

Bright Eyes
San Jose, Cuba

I was 8 years old and lived in an apartment complex with my parents. We lived in the last apartment building, which was pitch black at night, passed the building.

Well to this day I remember this vividly. I was always out playing with my friends and every single time it was time to go home I always ran. I ran because on the end of the building, where it was always dark, I always saw bright eyes staring at me. I didn't see anything just eyes.

I thought I didn't tell anyone else, but I was talking with

my mom a couple weeks back and I mentioned it to her. She told me one night I had told her and dad, they both ran outside to see who it was but found nothing. She even said my dad ran into the woods and nothing.

Obviously this isn't that scary like some of the stories in this app. But hell, this is the only weird thing that I experienced and can't explain.

The Bird
Santiago, Dominican Republic

This happened a long time ago. I was trying to go to sleep but I kept feeling a strange tickle in my feet. I opened my eyes and saw a little bird on my drawer. It had one red eye.

I got chills because all my windows were closed. Then I saw the bird outside my window. This was really weird because how could it teleport. So I got up and went outside. I could smell smoke. I heard a strange eerie laugh. I saw the bird on the ground and it burst into flames.

Then a man dressed in black and on fire was looking at me dead in the eye. He said "Nia ven conmigo" (Girl come with me). I screamed my lungs out. Then I just woke up at a hospital room. They said I had fainted.

Until this day I am scared of that. This is a true story.

Black Out
Santo Domingo, Dominican Republic

My family had recently moved to this island, which experiences blackouts all the time. My parents had left to go back to New York to take care of some business and left my sister and I alone with an older cousin.

It was around 8pm and the power had gone out, nothing out of the ordinary. I remember sitting at the dining table trying to learn my times table, I was 12 at the time. My sister and cousin were both helping me with my studies.

All of a sudden we saw this white figure start walking across the wall that was directly in front of us. It was bright white and had no characteristics other than a human form. We stared in horror. My cousin is a practicing evangelist and began shouting, "The power of Christ compels you!" in Spanish of course.

Immediately the ghost stopped in its tracks as if it were startled and ran, knocking the curtains off the glass doors leading to the balcony.

Well we were all so scared we all rushed to bed, and all three of us slept in our parents' bed.

The next morning we all awoke up at the same time and were shocked to see that the whole room was covered in what seem to be soot, like an ashy discharge commonly released from gas lamps. We ourselves were covered in it as well. We never owned a gas lamp.

This is not the last paranormal experience we had in this house, where a man hung himself on a mango tree, right where my dad built a guest room that is currently facing my room. But that was the first experience and it was one hell of an experience.

Take Care of My Children
Suwon City, South Korea

My friend Su-Gyung was 27 years old when she disappeared. She left behind a husband and two little boys. Her body was never found, but we presumed her to be dead after many months of searching.

In South Korea there is a tradition of remembering such people that have never been found. The day is September 9. Those who have lost loved ones visit empty memorial graves, burn incense, set out food, and recall special memories of their vanished loved ones. We have great respect for those who have passed on.

The dead, however, do not always share such respect for the living.

I married Su-Gyung's husband two years after Su-Gyung disappeared, and I adopted her two children as my own. By this time the oldest boy was eight. Now, before you judge me harshly, let me explain two things:

First, I never thought of Su-Gyung's husband that way until after she disappeared, leaving us heart-broken and searching for her.

And second, South Korea is a gentle place to raise children. Children are looked-after by the whole community. It is quite rare that anyone would intentionally harm a child. So, I thought nothing of it when I allowed the children to ride a bus by themselves across the city to see a movie. It was a quiet Sunday afternoon in March. I gave them money and a kiss, and sent them out.

This, however, would be the last time I ever neglected their safety.

I waited in worry just outside my front door at the top of the steps hour after hour for their return. Little did I know, the youngest had gotten lost, perhaps by getting off the bus at the wrong stop or perhaps by never getting on the bus in the first place. The oldest, only eight years old, searched the city frantically for his little brother and had no way to inform me.

Just at the moment I thought I could make out a couple of children on the next street corner, from behind me I felt the grip of a pair of ice-cold hands on my shoulders. Before I could prevent the inevitable, I was sent stumbling down the steps by an angry shove. In an instant I found myself suddenly face down on the sidewalk below.

Quickly curling up to grasp an oddly-twisted, scraped and throbbing ankle, I looked up to see my attacker. I didn't want to believe it, but there was absolutely no doubt. There above me stood a very angry, semi-transparent Su-Gyung frowning down on me from the top of the steps. Needless to say, I was terrified!

Using my already scuffed and bleeding palms, I drug myself backwards on the sidewalk for several feet until I was overcome with pain from the broken bone in my leg. At that very moment the two very anxious children came running up the sidewalk to me and threw their arms around me. They were home.

I quickly looked up at Su-Gyung again, but her spirit had vanished. She had delivered all the warning that would ever be necessary.

I spent the next four months attending physical therapy, and nearly two more months on a rigid exercise regime before I was able to fully recover physically. The very first morning I was able to stand up without any pain or discomfort was September 9. My husband and I took the children to their mom's memorial and spent the entire day there to pay honor to her memory.

Over the years Su-Gyung visited me three more times, but I never again gave her cause to question my ability to care for her children. She scolded me on each of the next two visits. Both times we had just recently moved into a new house, and both times she was upset that my husband's mother had been given the largest of the bedrooms. On her very last visit she gave me her blessing and said goodbye. After that I never saw her again. The two boys have grown to be such fine men now, and we continue to honor her memory each year.

Joe Kwon's True Ghost Stories

The Little Boys
Bluefields, Nicaragua

When I was 16 I went to Nicaragua where my mother was born. I spent a year learning Spanish since my family there only spoke Spanish. I was excited to go to another country since I had never left the States.

But what I would see would remain etched in my mind for the rest of my life.

The area in which we stayed was beautiful. My aunt lived in a beautiful plantation-style house. There were quite a few sugarcane fields that dominated most of the neighborhood where she lived.

It was July 22nd. I only remember the date because it was my grandma's birthday. The hot night began as any other. Everyone was eating, drinking, dancing, whatever goes on at a party. Later into the early hours of the morning my two cousins Connie and Roger, and I were hanging out in the yard talking. When suddenly we heard laughter coming from the front of the house, the laughter of children. Knowing that the three children of the house were asleep we dismissed it.

A few minutes later we heard it again. "Isn't it a little late for kids to be out?" I asked my cousin who nodded in agreement. We decided we would scare them since we were bored. We got our flashlights and proceeded to the front of the house. The laughter grew closer and we saw two little boys running and playing down the road. We

Volume 1 Ghost Stories from Around the World

decided we would hide and jump out at them to scare them... only it would be us who would be getting scared.

They got closer and closer, their laughter growing louder. "One. Two. Three!" We jumped out and turned our flashlights on and yelled, "What are you doing out so late!?" The boys were not startled, they looked up at us and my blood ran cold. I couldn't breathe and heard my pulse thumping loudly in my ear.

They stood there staring at us, no more laughter. Blood was dripping down their faces. One had almost half his face torn off. Blood poured from their shredded clothing, and one was missing the fingers of his right hand. There was a gurgled cry and then our flashlights died and the boys disappeared. As soon as the shock wore off we ran into the house in hysterics asking if we had all just seen the gruesome sight, hoping it was just one of ours' imagination. No, it was real.

Connie and I slept together that night. The laughter again came from the road in front of the house followed by the same gurgled scream. My heart was beating out of my chest and my stomach was in knots. Finally sleep managed to overcome me. The next morning we were eating breakfast while my aunt and grandma were watching tv. "Oh God, how horrible," I heard my aunt say. Connie, Roger and I got up to see what was on the tv that was so horrible. It was the news. They found two young boys mauled to death by wild dogs in one of the sugar cane fields. One was 10 the other 11 years old and they were killed two nights ago. They showed two side-by-side photos of the boys when they were alive. They were the same boys we saw the night before.

This happened five years ago, but the memories are as vivid as that night.

Stalking Headless Ghost Soldier
Occidental Mindoro, Philippines

First, before I tell and share my story let me give you a little history related to it. During the WWII, the time when Japanese tried to invade the Philippines, the soldiers were cruel and very brutal to people especially to Catholics, including priests being decapitated with their samurai. A lot of people suffered from tortures, rape, starvation, and killings. I remember my Granma telling me those stories of horror they went through at that time. She witnessed how Japanese soldiers killed her cousin and how he dug his own grave and how they decapitated his head. He was a member of the guerillas and killed a lot of Japanese soldiers during the rebellion. My story is not related to them actually, I just wanted readers to visualize it and have an idea how it was back then.

The land where our house was built is said to be one of the battlefields during the Japanese occupation. Many had died here. And since I was young I have seen a lot of strange occurrences here and up to now. I mean the most extreme ghost experiences you could ever imagine! (My third eye is strong and open by the way.) Ghosts NEVER go away. HERE ARE SOME OF MY EXPERIENCES:

Volume 1 Ghost Stories from Around the World

One late night, when I got home from my girlfriend's house, I got so tired and took a warm shower and jumped to my bed after. All of a sudden, when I was about to fell asleep, I smelled this strong sulfuric disgusting rotten sensation covering my whole room. It was that strong enough to give me a sick feeling in my stomach. So I got up and opened my windows to freshen up. The moon was bright and the air was refreshing. While I was opening the last two ones, that is when my horror started! What I saw was a horrifying scenery of Japanese soldiers in classic uniforms marching towards my room! I panicked in fear but I remember so clearly what they looked like: they were in squads of three and one of them in the first row had his face torn up, its flesh with bullet wounds on his rib cage, the next one had his shoulders hanging down like it was struck by a machete or some kind of sharp knife. It was swinging back and forth! My heart started to pump like hell! I thought to myself, "I know I've seen ghosts almost everyday, but please God not like this!" I ran quickly to get out of my room, but as I was about halfway through my door someone or something forcefully pushed it from behind! The pressure was so strong that I lost my balance and fell sitting on the floor. Still in shocked what it was, I still managed to look up and see only to find it was standing right in front of me! A bloody ghost soldier carrying his head on his right arm! I almost fainted right there but I couldn't take my eyes away from him! It was looking at me but his eyes were rolling in the opposite direction! I was so scared and helpless, I swear I felt like I was gonna die. Then the room started to get cold like it was freezing, the marching and the apparitions stopped and vanished finally.

The next morning I found myself on the floor. When I

recalled what had happened the night before, I almost cried in fear. You know the feeling of being helpless and at the same time the feeling of fighting your fear but don't know how? Cause I know what I'm dealing wasn't ordinary.

I thought it was over, I was wrong! That's when it started following me, the same ghost with the decapitated head. Up to this day, he still follows me in the house like he is trying to communicate with me but all he does is to scare me. Like one time, I was watching TV, his head will appear over the shelf and his body will be on my side before I know it! I always feel sick every time I see him. I hope this will end soon before I lose my sanity.

My Older Sister's Daughter
Stockholm, Sweden

My sister, Natalie, and her boyfriend Oswald moved in together. My sis was 15 years old. Oswald was 17. Oswald was so nice until he got my sis pregnant. She was 14 at the event. She felt awfully sick. She went to the doctor, and found out she was pregnant.

Oswald seemed like a different person after that, so was Natalie. I was 8 at the time. A year later was when Oswald moved in with her. Their baby was healthy. Her name was Kayleigh.

Natalie turned 17. Her birthday present was a ring from Oswald. She accepted. Shorty after that, a couple months later, she was pregnant again! Kayleigh was 3 at the time. A couple of months later two baby boys (natural twins) were born, Austin and Markus. It was December 14th.

Kayleigh went out to experience snow. Oswald was supposed to supervise her while Natalie was nursing the boys. Oswald went in to get a coke and came out and Kayleigh was gone. He didn't know what to do. He saw a collapsed tunnel. He was holding back tears as he started brushing snow out of the way. Kayleigh surprisingly survived. They rushed her to the hospital immediately. The doctor diagnosed her with Hypothermia. And she had a slight heart problem. A couple weeks later she died of Hypothermia.

Oswald never told Natalie what really happened. He told her she got out the back door. He didn't want to lose Natalie. Natalie and Oswald always saw Kayleigh walking around in the kitchen smiling. Natalie never had another child again. After Austin and Markus became 8 years old they would talk to Kayleigh with an Ouija board. She would never do anything violent. She would always say, "I love you" to them.

One day Natalie and Oswald played with them, and Kayleigh hugged Natalie and Oswald. And said "I love you" but then she said the doctors gave her a needle and her heart started getting sharp pains and she started falling asleep. After the story Natalie and Oswald were in tears. But she said she was happy. And she said there really is a Heaven.

But then she mentioned being left outside with no help...

The Black Shadow
Venice, Lido di Valencia Italy

Well I was on a school trip. We were in Venice. We stayed at a Hotel called Hotel Cristalo. I shared a room with my three good friends Adele, Sveva, and Eleonora.

One night I could hear voices. My three friends were asleep. I could hear these sounds very faintly when I closed my eyes. When I was looking outside of the window I saw this black figure at the corner of my eye. I turned my head swiftly and now I saw what had attracted my attention. It was a dark figure with a hood looking down at my best friend sleeping, Eleonora. I was staring at it in horror. In a split second the black hooded figure turned at looked straight at me. Then it vanished.

Silent Stranger
Aberdeen, Aberdeenshire Scotland

I've always believed in things that seemed unnatural or paranormal, I would love hearing ghost stories from friends and would sit for hours listening as they relayed their stories to me. It wasn't about the scare so much, it was more about the mystery and the why of things. So when things started happening to me I wasn't exactly terrified.

Anyway, for years I have been on the receiving end of weird things happening, nothing like the exorcist or poltergeist but they were always questionable things. They started when I was just a child, I would wake up screaming in the middle of the night in absolute fear. I would wake to find a face hovering over me just staring at me, hollow eyes and a mouth parted slightly, almost as if they were about to start a conversation or ask me a question. Other times I would wake to find the same face with body sitting on the end of my bed just staring as usual. This went on for a few years and then suddenly stopped.

Although I never saw the face again I would always get chills, the horrible feeling of someone walking over your grave and the uncomfortable feeling of being watched. Then as I got into my teens it was small things that would happen, I would be sitting at the computer listening to music and would hear someone calling my name, when I would question my mum or dad about it they would deny calling on me. It always sounded like the voice was echoing in my head, it sometimes sounded male and sometimes sounded female. It was usually when I was listening to music but on a few occasions it would happen when I was sitting by myself. I would be walking home from school and it would feel like someone was following me, or when I was walking from a friend's house.

I live in a flat with my parents and brother, I'm 21 and have lived there all my life, I've never known the history of the flat so I was surprised to have a dream about my room being on fire, the walls were peeling with the heat and it was so hot and there was a little boy just staring at me. The next day I spoke to my mum and for some reason asked her if there had been a fire in the house, she gave me a weird look and then told me that there had been a fire in my bedroom years ago before her and my dad moved in. Two boys were at home by themselves because their mum was on a night out and a fire started, although my mum said no one had died.

And about a year ago I woke up from a deep sleep to once again find a face hovering above me, it was a man with hollow eyes and white hair brushed back. He didn't look threatening but did look a little freaky. Being tired I blinked slowly and turned over to fall asleep once again.

Then a few months back I was at the cinema with my friend and her sister, the film had yet to start so we were sitting having a chat. We were at the back and behind us were the premier seats, there was just a piece of rope blocking it off. I turned slightly listening to my friend talk about the film when I saw someone in the premier row of seats standing beside the rope, it was a bit dull so I couldn't see exactly who it was, he started walking behind me and when I looked again he was gone. I thought it had been someone who worked in the cinema checking things out but there was no one behind us, but then I realized it was the same man I'd seen staring down at me months earlier. My friends were totally freaked out and said I attracted weird stuff.

On my way home that night I swear there was someone behind me following me but they had my exact shadow. The two mingled together like whoever was behind me was running to catch up and when I turned round no one was there. About a week afterwards I told my friend at work who is a spiritual healer and the like and as I was talking about what happened one of the ring binders on our desk which was right in the center flipped off the table and landed on the floor.

A few weeks ago I woke up again to find the same man at the edge of my bed just staring at me again and every night I get a tingle like someone is sitting next to my leg before I fall asleep.

I don't know who this man is or what he wants but it's got me a little frightened, not because of his presence but more of why he is there. Does he want to communicate? Or is he just looking over me? Who knows, I may never find out.

Slapping Poltergeist
Legal, Alberta Canada

Every town has its ghost stories. As children, the "haunted house" in town scared us as well as drew us. I'm sure everyone can relate to this feeling.

As a child, my sister and I lived at the top of town. Legal is built over a small valley. We would often go by this small house on the way home to our aunt's. She was the one who first said it was haunted. She told me stories of kids in the 80's (we were 90's kids) that went in and never came out. This house was the typical "haunted house." Always dark inside, crappy looking exterior, old 50's style design. A house you could believe inhabited spectres. Until they built the KC ball diamond near it, and more houses in the next few years, it was on the outskirts of town.

Some of my friends and I often played around it to prove we weren't scared. We were 10 years old and ballsy. One time a man's voice shouted "GET OFF MY LAWN!" There was no one around. This house had no neighbors. Damn, did we hop on our bikes and bolt! Time goes on and we're there again. We weren't scared (yeah right), and this time we're looking in the windows. It's bright day, and a little light is on in the house. My friend Shawn saw something and screamed. We ran to his side of the house, and his pants were soaked (he peed his pants), and he was crying hysterically. We walked him home, and he never told us what he saw. He would always be scared to speak of it.

About a year later, we grew brave enough to throw rocks through the windows, to get back at the ghosts. After that, every one of us that threw rocks got nasty sunburns with deep green bruises in them. We got sick way more easily too.

We decided not to let it beat us. We were running around it at night. We were pushing whatever was there to act against us. I stopped running and turned around on the grass, looking at the house. I saw something white move from the left window on the second floor, to the right very quickly. My friend Nathan was just rounding the house coming towards me. The white thing moved from the right room of the second floor to outside the house at ground level and I heard something like a slap, and Nathan fell over.

The white thing went into the ground as Craig was coming around the house, and he ran to Nathan. As he bent down to Nathan, the window on the second floor shattered and we heard a man scream, "GET AWAY!" This all happened within 3 - 5 seconds, so the ghost was incredibly fast.

We never went back. The ghost had won. We told our parents, but they didn't believe us. However, they also quickly wrote off our requests for them to go check it out. I think they were just as scared as us.

There are actually people living there now, who have been there for the better part of a decade. I'm wondering how they did it. Ghosts don't just leave. Maybe they came to a compromise or something. Who knows? All I know is that house freaked me out, and even when I biked to the KC diamond for baseball practice or games, I gave it a wide berth.

I'm 25 now. I look back at the situation from a more mature standpoint, and I wouldn't change my experience a bit. It was fun.

Ghost Bruises in Sweden
Trollhattan, Alvsborg Sweden

This story was told to me when I was a little boy by my late grandmother, Annie, who migrated to this country in the 1890's.

She lived near a cemetery and wanted to take some flowers off some of the graves, but her mother forbade her from doing so. Annie (who was around nine or ten then) was told she must never disturb the sleep of the dead or they would take revenge.

Of course, some time later Annie did as she was told not to do, and made up a story about picking the flowers along the roadside. Her mother was not fooled and accused Annie of taking flowers from a grave. "Look! The spirits have marked you for your sin!" she cried. On Annie's right bicep were bruises in the form of fingerprints as though someone had gripped it with superhuman force. Her mother commanded my grandmother to put the flowers back where she found them immediately. Frightened, Annie did so, and upon arriving back home...there were no bruises.

Annie shook her head as she told me this. "Yah, sure, dere vas ghosts dere, all right!"

My Son Came to Say Goodbye!
Misawa, Aomori Japan

While stationed in Japan, I encountered this experience.

I was 8 months pregnant with my 3rd child, a boy. It was a very stressful pregnancy, due to complications, and the fact that I never felt that I would ever have the baby home with me. Finally one night, while lying in bed with my husband, I told him my feelings.

I just knew in my heart that we would never bring Zachary home, as we had named him. I could never picture him being a physical part of our lives. My husband of course, told me I was insane! He didn't believe me. One night about a week later, while asleep in my bed, I woke up to the sound of a child crying! I must say, I was used to getting up in the middle of the night, as my young daughter woke me up quite regularly.

When I sat up in bed, immediately I noticed a small child standing inside my bedroom at my door. The child wore only a diaper. At the time, I was so focused on checking on my little girl that I just assumed it was her. I remember the child so well, it had really dark brown hair, and wore only a diaper. It stood in my doorway and looked directly at me. I saw it as clear as day!

I jumped up and ran into the hall and into my daughter's room, and she was sound asleep in her bed, as was my eldest son! Immediately I realized that I had just ran straight through the apparition, and turned to look at it. It faded right before my eyes. I was shocked to say the least. I jumped back into bed, and covered my head with the covers!

About a week later I had a similar experience, but this time I just woke up out of a sound sleep. Standing next to me, beside my bed, was the same little boy, this time he was wearing a red plaid shirt. When the time came to have my baby, unfortunately, due to negligence on the part of the physicians treating me, I lost my child during labor.

I never did get to bring him home, although I did get to tell him bye, and how much I loved him. I must say he was truly beautiful. He had the darkest brown hair. He was the only one of my babies to have brown hair. He was a big baby too. I wonder, did he come back to tell his mama bye-bye? I think he did!

Woman in White
Auckland, New Zealand

This took place at Shakespeare Lodge in April. I was 11 years old at the time and I was playing a game with my friends in the forest with a parent.

While we were playing I suddenly stopped. I had seen something or someone in the distance. I was frozen, I stood there until my friends called up to me to come out of the forest. When I was out and was sitting on a log I saw it again, this time I could see it more clearly. It was a woman dressed in a white long dress and had a bunch of flowers in her hand.

I turned away, but I couldn't help looking back. This time she was standing in a different position, it felt like she was looking at me. I didn't tell anyone around me I thought they would think I was crazy.

After that experience I do not want to go back there again.

The Lost Tiki
Port Waikato, Auckland New Zealand

This story is about the lost tiki and was told to me by my aunt, my dad's sister in-law.

The event took place in the early 70's when my aunt was 3. She lived on a farm with her parents, her Uncle Roy, her older sister and baby brother who was barely walking.

Uncle Roy had only just moved in at the time. It was especially exciting for the kids to have someone else around as they rarely had visitors.

A few weeks later, Uncle Roy received mail from an unknown sender, no address, no stamp, no letter, just his name. Inside is an emerald stone tiki. It's larger than most you'll find nowadays, and these particular tiki stones are family heirlooms.

Uncle Roy is the eldest of 7 and his father was also the eldest amongst his siblings and so on. As part of the Maori lore, the eldest of every generation is to take care of the tiki till the day they pass. But, if the tiki is passed down to the wrong person very dangerous events will occur.

One day, my Aunt Marilyn and her older sister were playing outside when all of a sudden they heard their mother scream, and without thinking they both stopped what they were doing and ran inside, to find their baby brother crawling up the walls. By the time he got to the ceiling their father ran in with a ladder and managed to get him down.

That wasn't the only horrifying incident, from then on there was a constant chill in the house, the family experienced terrible nightmares every night which resulted in lack of sleep, they constantly heard strange voices, were violently attacked by unseen forces and were generally scared for their lives. All of these terrible things happened to everyone but Uncle Roy.

My aunt's mother Linda demanded that Uncle Roy get rid of the tiki, as that was the only negative object she could think of that might be the reason for the horrible disturbances. Uncle Roy saw how this was affecting the family and knew it was the only way... but getting rid of it wasn't as easy as they thought it was.

That same night Uncle Roy threw it in the bin outside, but as soon as he walked back in he found it sitting on his drawer. After two more attempts, the tiki somehow always found its way back on the drawer.

Next day he made a trip to the bank in an attempt to lock it in the bank vault... only to find it sitting on the kitchen bench, at home.

Later that afternoon Uncle Roy planned to go fishing with his mates from the pub, in another attempt to be rid of the tiki. Uncle Roy told his mates about the tiki. They all laughed it off and told him he's crazy. One of his mates offered to throw it away to make sure it won't run away, to add to the humor.

Volume 1 Ghost Stories from Around the World

Two hours later, they headed back to shore. On the way home Uncle Roy was restless, eager to get home... only to find the tiki on the kitchen bench once again.

Next morning the phone rang, my aunt's father answered the phone and was told that an awful accident had happened to a mate of Uncle Roy's... yes, the same mate that tossed the tiki into the sea. He died from 3rd degree burns while he was asleep, yet there was no fire detected anywhere near him or his home.

The more Uncle Roy tried to dispose of the tiki the worse things got around the house, even to the point where my aunt's sister and father were rushed to hospital.

In a desperate bid to find answers, Uncle Roy phoned all of relatives but had no luck, none of them sent the tiki nor knew who sent it.

Things were getting worse. He was helpless and scared for their lives.

In a rage he grabbed the tiki and marched outside and picked up the axe, placed the tiki on the stump and hurled the axe into the tiki... to his surprise he didn't even leave a scratch on the tiki. Over and over he kept at it but no luck.

Next, he prepared a bonfire, lit it up and threw the tiki in. For the next 10 minutes he kept a close eye on it to make sure it didn't move anywhere. As the fire burned vigorously, the tiki remains intact. Several hours later Uncle Roy went to check on it but this time noticed something below one of the eyes of the tiki. It appeared to be in the shape of a tear drop. It was getting late so he decided to go to bed after a long night.

Next morning, everyone in the house seems happy and in a good mood and discussed how they slept extremely well after two very terrible months. Suddenly Uncle Roy ran outside to see if the tiki was still in amongst the ash, only to find nothing but ash.

He searched the house high and low, inside and outside... and still no sign of it.

Weeks later they were phoned by an aunt from down south, telling them how their father had a son before Uncle Roy, but with another woman! Uncle Roy felt more relieved and didn't think it was strange when they mentioned that this half brother had received the tiki by mail two weeks ago!

Uncle Roy died peacefully several years later. My aunt would happily say that when people asked him about the tiki he would say the tiki was only trying to find his way home and we were the bloody dumb Maoris standing in its way!

Moving Shadow
Manama, Bahrain

I was in bed when I heard a rattling. I thought it was just my mother going to get a drink or something, so I ignored it. This rattling carried on for several minutes, so I thought I better go see. I took a tennis racket, which I kept in my cupboard, just for protection. The noise was coming from the bathroom. All the lights in the house were off except for my bedroom one, and one in the hall that supplied a little light in the bathroom.

I slowly opened the door and I was saying "hello, mum?!" then the rattling stopped.

I looked inside and I could see a shadow in the corner by the shower. At first I thought it was nothing, but then it moved towards me. I quickly turned the light on, but there was nothing. One thing I noticed was that the room was considerably colder than out in the hall, and there were no windows open. I'm not sure if this is of any use, but it is the truth.

Dia de los Muertos (Day of the Dead)
Tijuana, Baja California Mexico

This incident happened in 2006 and it was what in the Hispanic culture is called the Days of the Dead, from November 1st to the 3rd. Each of those days is dedicated to on one day one celebrates children, another all the saints, and the dead have free reign to visit, and the other for adults.

I was there as an American woman going to med school there, and at the time my 5 year old son Aidan was living with me and I would drop him off at a close friends' to spend the night while I had a study group to attend to at 10 pm that night

As I got into my car, a little Nissan, I leaned down to put my purse on the passengers seat, I came back and was putting on my seatbelt and looked up to the road and in the distance I saw a man coming and got nervous. I didn't want to get robbed, so I turned the car on and drove forward.

The man I saw was wearing blue jeans, a black windbreaker, a red baseball cap and had a black backpack. As I got closer to him I thought he would walk towards the sidewalk or else I would run him over, but no, he kept walking steadily. So I slowed down and honked at him. Then he just moved enough for me to get by. I then looked at him and opened my window half way to cuss at him (stupid move). He looked right at me and I stared at his face and his eyes were completely BLACK, no whites, nada!!

I was so close to him that if I reached I could have touched him, I saw him so clearly then I thought he was probably just trying to scare people on this night and put on those weird contact lenses to scare the crap out of people.

I was trying to rationalize this when I looked to my rear

view mirror was what scared me like nothing else.

I looked and the young man was staring at me still but you see he was walking away from my car but his head was turned ALL THE WAY AROUND like the exorcist but he was smiling.

Weirdly I stayed calm and kept driving and tried not to focus on what happened. I got to my study group's meeting place and no one was there. I called one of the group's members who told me, "Hell no! No one really goes out on these nights! Who knows what one will see!" Then I said, "No sh**!"

But had to go get my son and I had to pretend like nothing (for my sanity) happened while I walked to the door. Once in I ran and told the babysitter and she said, "Only Americanos go out like this and never respect the dead!"

The Old Man vs. The Boy
Bayaman, Puerto Rico

When I was a little girl I used to stay awake until would come walking around my bed an old man dressed in white with a long white beard. He walked with a cane and very slowly he entered my room, walked around my bed and stared at me. For me, this was perfectly fine. I felt in peace and ready to go to sleep. This went on for a couple of months.

One night, as usual, I was waiting for my visitor to make his ritual but it was taking a little bit more time for him to show up. I was getting a little anxious and kept on looking to the door. Suddenly, I felt a cold chill And pulled up my blanket. I remember that only my eyes were showing. Then the most terrifying thing happened. I heard a sound coming from the right corner of the room. I looked from the floor up. I saw two black shoes; they were small. I kept on looking up and saw long white socks. I saw light gray shorts and a white shirt. I saw a stain in his shirt. Kept looking up and saw his face, pale, sad. It was a small boy. But on his head down to his left eyebrow I saw a huge amount of blood. I just lied there, terrified and just couldn't talk or scream. Then, he came floating with straight arms toward me. That's when I sat up on my bed and cried for help waking up my parents.

Needless to say, that after that night I slept for a couple of weeks with my parents and even stopped seeing the old man at night.

Volume 1 Ghost Stories from Around the World

Baby Boy Aged 2
Luton, Bedfordshire England

I am telling this story on behalf of my dad. This didn't happen to me it happened to my dad when he was in his mid twenties.

My dad agreed to babysit for his friends one Saturday night. So he turns up at 6, says bye to his friends who say they won't be home late, and starts playing with all the children.

Anyway, after food and bath all the children are tired and my dad puts them to bed. Two girls in one room, the little boy in the other.

Dad checks on them after about 30 minutes. All the kids are sleeping so Dad gets comfy watching tv.

About an hour or so later he hears a thumping noise from upstairs. Thinking one of them has gotten out of bed Dad checks but all are asleep.

Later he hears a child laughing and babbling away. He goes upstairs ready to put the child back to bed, but when he looks in the rooms they are all asleep.

As my dad is turning to come downstairs he hears laughing from the bathroom. He opens the door and there is a little boy sitting on the potty laughing to himself.

My dad just backs away, not believing his eyes because he's just checked all three children are in bed. He waits downstairs for his friends to return.

Once home my dad tells them what happened and the mum bursts out crying. Turns out that before the oldest child was born they had a baby boy who died, aged 2.

Hello? Who is Calling?
Bedok, Reservoir Singapore

I don't want to talk about this anymore, however, I feel like sharing it.

Five days ago I was at home alone, suddenly the door of my room were closed. I thought that it was the wind so again I opened the door. Three minutes after the incident my home phone rang.

"Hello? Hello? Who's this?" I replied. What I said earlier.

Then all of the sudden my hand phone rang. "Hello, Janice is that you? Hello?"

Janice is my best friend, and likes to disturb me. I suspected that she is the one who was doing this.

Without movement from me, the door closed again. The kitchen, toilet, living room and my siblings and parents' room doors and lights all closed too! I take this serious. I, myself opened the door and shouted, "Who's that?"

Volume 1 Ghost Stories from Around the World

I opened the lights and doors, and when I was going to open the toilet door, I felt something warning me not to. My heart was pulling me backwards. My heart was paying full attention to it. I thought no ghost will exist, so I opened the toilet door and I saw a lot of blood floating.

My home phone rang. Cold tears ran on my cheeks. I hoped is my mother, but... suddenly my hand phone rang too. I was too scared to pick up, when I tell myself it's mom with private number calling me. I pick up and heard a ghostly sound talking on the line. "Rachel, Rachel, you are the only one who can see my blood, hear me, feel me. Last time the toilet of yours was my garden, my best friend name Annie Lim were jealous of my beauty, she brought me to the garden and tied me up, and she strangle me to death. She hung me up the tree because she wants peoples to think I hang myself. Help me, by going to the toilet, and take a red dress and red lipstick and shoes. Burn it to me then I won't disturb you again. If you don't I am coming to take you away."

I was very scared, and how does she know my name? Why doesn't my mom know about this? I did what she said, I was terrified. Imagine you are my shoes. From that day onwards, I, myself, never stayed at home alone.

Unexplainable
Gstaad, Bern Switzerland

This only happened to me early this morning. I am eleven years old and this really isn't a ghost story but it's definitely what I can call unexplainable.

I woke up to hear the television on and continuously changing channels. At first I thought it was one of my parents because they don't always sleep the whole night through. I was too scared to go and check so I just passed it off as nothing and went back to sleep.

The 2nd time I woke up I heard what sounded like my dog drinking from her water bowl but she was sleeping right next to me. And the television was still running. I was starting to get a little freaked our. And the 3rd time I woke up and my dog was barking at nothing and she wouldn't stop no matter how much I tried to stop her.

The weird thing is I just was researching Ouija boards yesterday. Please tell me what this could be.

Ghostly Strength
Eagle Base, Bosnia

I am an active-duty Army soldier. It was in March that my unit was deployed to Bosnia. After I got here, I heard the locals talk about how haunted the woods were, among other places. As usual, I lent no importance to what these people were saying.

The event happened to me less than a week after my arrival. I was sleeping in my seahut. (A seahut is a one-story building that houses eight to twelve men). I was awakened by the physical sensation of someone running their hands over my blankets. Seeing nothing, I passed that off as a fluke and fell back to sleep.

Then, the dream that I had did not help the situation. To save time I will condense it... I dreamed my family and I had gotten into an argument at a restaurant. I told them that I was leaving and going back home. For some reason in the restaurant was my luggage, and it was too much for one trip. I picked up what I could and carried it to my truck.

Upon my return, there was a man in the restaurant and his skin was totally white, and he was wearing an even whiter vest and his left hand was perfectly sliced off. He had no facial features. He looked like a Barbie doll with no color.

I awoke from this dream in a cold sweat. I lay in bed looking at the ceiling. I was not awake more than a couple of seconds when a fear that froze me came over my body.

I sleep with the covers over my head (don't ask me why). I tried to speak but I could not utter a single word even though I tried my hardest. Then, the blankets slowly were pulled from over my head down to the center of my chest. This made me even more scared and yet I could neither move nor talk. It felt like minutes but I'm sure only a few seconds had passed before the blankets started to move again.

Somehow I got the nerve to grab the blanket with the only hand that would function. I gripped and tried to pull the blanket back to my face. But I was met with a force that was much stronger than me because it ripped the blanket from my hand and pulled it past my waist.

I am no small man. I am six feet, one-inch and weigh 195 pounds. Whatever it was that pulled the blanket from my hand was stronger then me.

A couple of minutes had gone by, and slowly I regained the ability to move. Once that happened, I shot out of bed to notice that my clock was frozen at exactly 1 a.m. But, none of my other roommates' clocks had any problems at all.

I left the seahut and went to the rec center to recall the whole incident, which I wrote down. I am very hard to scare Very. But, whatever happened to me this night put the fear of God in me.

Ghost in the Backyard
Brunei-Muara, Brunei Darussalam Borneo

This was actually happened to my brother and my grandmother. It was about 8:30 pm when my grandmother and my brother went out to the backyard to put out the fire.

My brother was carrying a kettle full of water and a torch light. As they got closer to the fire, they saw this figure all in white moving towards their torchlight. As they moved backwards, the figure continued to get closer to them. Then both of them realized that the figure was a ghost.

Without thinking, my brother ran as quickly as he can leaving my grandmother behind. I was in the kitchen when this happened. My brother knocked the kitchen door very hard and when I opened the door, he crushed onto me. Then when I asked him about grandmother, he said that he had left her alone in the backyard. Then I saw my grandmother running for the door but did not see the ghost. She was as frightened as he was.

Frightening Wake Up
Varna, Bulgaria

I was in Bulgaria and I was staying near the beach. I was 10 years old at the time. I was sitting on my bed in the old bungalow I was staying in.

My cousin was reading a book about ghosts and spirits.

I laid down on the bed and fell asleep immediately, as I was very tired from the beach trip that we had had earlier on in the day.

I woke up. I gasped. I was in my Gran's bed in her flat. I looked around. It seemed to be daytime. The door opened and my Gran came in. I was very afraid, as I knew this was really happening. I looked around again and I saw that I was see through.

I screamed and felt myself fainting. I woke up again in the bungalow near the beach. My cousin looked at me strangely. I asked her if anything weird had happened. She said no, the only weird thing was that I seemed pretty disturbed when I was sleeping.

Later I told her about what happened. She gasped and looked at her book. "I read that your spirit sometimes comes out of your body and goes somewhere else. But no one sees you because you're not in your body. Meanwhile your body seems dead as there is nobody inside it."

This was probably what had happened to me. Hmmm. What do you think?

Spirit Confused By Instant Death
Eureka, California USA

Five years ago I worked in a facility for the mentally ill in Eureka, California. I worked closely with two good friends and fellow coworkers Rhonda and Holly. After a long shift one Friday night, Rhonda, Holly, and I parted ways for the weekend.

Saturday night, Rhonda and I both received phone calls that our friend Holly died in a car accident. The details were short, she was hit in a head on collision and died instantly. Rhonda, myself, and fellow coworkers consoled each other that weekend. We talked about Holly and how she had the loudest laugh, how she always told the best jokes, and how when she was mad, she would stomp off.

We continued work Monday as usual, distraught by Holly's sudden and instant death. Wednesday at work, Rhonda had a chilling story to tell me. She was sleeping late at night. Around 3 a.m., she was awakened to sobbing. She sat up in her bed and saw Holly crouched on the corner of her bedroom crying. Stunned, Rhonda took a second to gather herself, then she spoke to Holly. Rhonda said, "Holly, you died." Rhonda could not understand what Holly said after that but it was short and Rhonda gathered that Holly was worried about her daughter. Rhonda replied, "She will be ok, your mom will take care of her."

Holly spoke again saying, "I don't know what is happening." Rhonda knew that Holly was confused and did not realize that she was dead. Holly died so suddenly that she most likely did not realize what had happened. Rhonda again told Holly that she died in a car accident and she needed to go where she belonged, she needs to go to the light.

Then, all Rhonda could hear were foot steps stomping off, just like Holly did when she was mad. I get chills thinking about it to this day. But no one has had any Holly encounters since. Rest in peace friend.

Risen
Casa, Casa Morocco

I am sorry for my English ... but I hope you all will understand it.

Every member of my friend's family has seen him risen above his bed for about 1 meter. And this happened many times ... another friend of ours, when he was camping with him, saw him in the morning risen above his bed...

More... he always saw some people in his room ... and some times he heard them calling his name ... and also he switched off the light, and when he woke up in the morning he found the light switched on.

There is also many others stories about my friend. There is also a web site from Emirate of my friend and what happened with his ghost.

Journey Out Of My Body
Tarragona, Catalynya Spain

I was asleep in my bed dreaming and I woke up, but everywhere around my body was tingling and I felt like I was falling. I could not move or speak. I was trying to move my arm but I could not.

I could see my room and everything around me, but in the corner of my room I saw a black hole that should not be there, and I saw spiders coming out the hole charging towards me. And I had this terrible feeling that if I let the spiders get to me something terrible would happen.

But it was too late, the spiders got me. Then everything went black. After a couple of seconds I heard this big bang, and suddenly I was on the ceiling looking down at my body. And then suddenly I was flying through the sky and again everything went black, and I woke up back in my tingling body.

The whole experience felt very real, and at first it was

very frightening, but then it felt like excitement and freedom. But it has never happened again. So far.

Respiratory Therapist
Bacoor, Cavite Philippines

I am a new nurse in a 130+ bed Hospital in Bacoor Cavite, Philippines.

There's a ramp mostly used in case of emergency that I always use to go to 4th floor. "A little exercise for me," I said. But, whenever I used the ramp to get to the second floor, I always felt weird. I felt that someone was behind me laughing. It was feeling of tightness & coldness, and it was so intense that I always ended up running.

One day, my supervisor sent me to work on the second floor for the 10pm - 6am shift. Me and one tech were the only ones working that night in that unit. We had six patients. My tech was going to come to work late, and the afternoon shift already left, so I started the shift alone.

It was my usual habit to begin each shift by wiping my work place with alcohol wipes. As I was doing this, I heard footstep from the hallway. I look to see if my tech had arrived, but instead I saw a man dressed in RT scrubs walking through the hall accompanied by two women chatting behind him.

I was not wearing my eyeglasses at the time, so my vision was a little blurred. I could tell from his face that he was

47

looking and smiling at me, so I smiled back.

Then, I looked down again at what I was doing, only to suddenly realize one thing... I could see right through him! Why did I have perfect vision of the women behind him... their dresses, figures and actions? I immediately looked up again. No one was there, but the ICU door that was just in font of my unit just opened and then closed. I immediately knew something was wrong, but I didn't believe in ghosts... so I went ahead to investigate.

The man and women I had seen could not be found. I found the ICU nurse on duty and told her what I had seen, and she reported it to the supervisor.

Later on, a tech and I were working on that floor again. During my shift, the house supervisor began telling us about a Respiratory Therapist who used to work at night on that floor, and about how he was usually assigned to ICU. He usually stayed in the room underneath the ramp between the 1st and 2nd floor (where I would get the intense feeling of being watched). One night he passed away there in that room in his sleep.

After learning of this, I observed even more strange things occurring on that floor-- in both the ER and in ICU. Fans and lights would turn on and off, doors would open and close, and water faucets would turn on and shut off. It became so frequent that it was actually as annoying as it was scary.

Finally, on November 1 (All Saints Day), it came to a climax. Everything seemed to happen all at once. And, I encountered the apparition again...

There were three patients in my unit on the 2nd floor, and there was one patient in ICU. The ICU patient was not able to breathe on his own and had to be connected to a respirator to keep him alive. Of course, the lights suddenly went off and we realized we had to hurry to the ICU to manually respirate the patient or he could die within seconds.

We quickly ran to the ICU to save him. But, when we arrived at the doorway to the ICU, what we saw was beyond comprehension. The apparition was there in the dark, leaning over the patient attempting to manually ambu-bag the patient to keep him alive. Fortunately, within seconds the electricity came back on and the apparition vanished.

We prayed so hard, like never before, telling him to move on, telling him that he was dead.

Next day we went to his tomb and offer a prayer for his soul again. The RT room was blessed that week and reopened again. After that, the second floor looks more warm, more fresh and definitely bright as if it's the first time light has ever reached that floor.

Business Trip Nightmare
Chennai, India

I have traveled all over the world with my job. Although I

am a young female, I have never worried about traveling on my own, even in places like India. I love India and its people and always felt welcome on my trips to the Tamil region.

On one trip I had to take a flight to Delhi via Chennai to meet a supplier. I stayed in Chennai for the night before my connecting flight in the morning. I was tired and was relieved to reach the apartment that had been provided by my business partners in India.

It was late evening and dark when I arrived. The apartment was of a good standard, but there was a water shortage and the electric supply kept going off. I went to my room and read for a while. The air was heavy and very hot, and I slept on and off.

Then sometime in the night I awoke with a start! There were hands gripping me tightly around my ankles! I was slowly being dragged off the bed! I started to panic, and my heart was beating rapidly now. I tried to kick and thrash around, and I could not see my attacker! I tried to grab hold of the mattress but was being pulled off the bed.

Just then the grip released. I was free! I didn't want to move or breathe, and was absolutely terrified. I decided to make a run for it. I still couldn't see my attacker, as it was so dark. But I decided I needed to get out of the apartment fast.

I ran for the door and into the living area. It was so quiet. Just then the electricity kicked in and all the lights came on. I stopped dead in my tracks. There was nobody following me. I stood still, glancing around for what must be about 30 seconds. I could hear or see nothing, so decided to glance into my room. There was nothing or nobody there. My window was closed and when I inspected it, it was shut tight with screws.

I sat on a chair trying to make sense of what had happened. I was still convinced that something would jump out at any moment. I never slept again that night. And my attacker did not reveal itself. I really don't know what to make of what happened. I had red marks on my ankles, which turned into light bruises in the days that followed.

It didn't stop me traveling, but I did have other experiences on other business trips. Will post my other true story if you are interested.

Sail Away
Belfast, Co. Antrim Ireland

Well I can't say I never really believed in ghosts, because this situation happened to me when I was just 9 years old. I always had bad nightmares even from a very young age. My mum and dad were always very good about it, putting me back down to sleep and making me feel better. But on this one occasion I did not need them to come into my room, as the boy I had been dreaming about for many years did!

On the night in question I was seeing things in my room: the walls came in towards me and the wallpaper slowly came to life. An over-active imagination, perhaps, but still happening to me, none the less.

I slowly drifted off to sleep. Again a boy in the sailor suit woke me up -- the same boy who died by falling of the roof in my dreams almost every night for 2 years! I always woke up at the same time, just as he hit the ground. The next day after the hallucinations I had in my room, I was telling my mum, if I could just try to catch him before he falls, he might just go away and leave me alone. That night I eventually fell asleep with the usual hallucinating, determined to try and catch the boy who tortured my dreams.

Again I was awakened when the young boy fell of the large slate roof to his death. Not put off by this, only my first attempt at saving him, I tried every night that week to put an end to my nightmare. And, continued each night without success.

On the last of the nights in that week, I was getting ready for bed. The light in the hall was on, but I only had my night light on in my room. When I turned to get into bed, my door only slightly ajar, I saw him coming from the bathroom at the end of the hall, right up the hallway, and into my room. Totally speechless, the boy in the sailor suit just walked up to my bed, looked at me, smiled, and calmly walked on through my window and out of my room.

I went to bed (eventually) and I never dreamed of that boy again after that night. A few weeks after it happened, my mum and I were talking to my great Grandad who at the time was 96. And he said at the time the houses where we live were being built, maybe 70 years before, there was a young boy who died during the construction. And without me telling him, he said I believe he was wearing a white and blue sailor suit. He was just seven years old when he died.

A Mexican Haunting
Nueva Rosita, Coahuila Mexico

When I was about 4 years old, my family and I went to Mexico for my mom's cousin's wedding. We went, had a great time, and the time came for us to leave. We didn't have a hotel room so my mom's cousin offered her home to my parents and I. She said we could have her room and she would sleep with her daughters in their room.

Since I was so little, I slept in the middle of the bed with my parents. My dad and I were the first ones to fall asleep. My mom stayed up to take off her contacts and wash off her makeup. Once she was done, she crawled into bed with us and lied there. The bed was facing the doorway. Since my mom had taken off her contacts and she had her glasses under her pillow, she could not see clearly.

While she was staring at the doorway, she said that she noticed someone peeking into the room. When she would call out if anyone was there, the head would disappear. When she looked away, she noticed the head peeking in again out of the corner of her eye. She called out again, this time she called out her cousin's name, thinking she was probably checking up on us. What happened next, she could not explain how or even why.

She was sleeping with her arms over her head and her legs crossed at the ankles. All of a sudden she felt someone grab her ankles and uncross her legs and hold them down. Her arms that were over her head were also uncrossed and held down on the bed. At that exact moment, according to my mom, my dad and I started making strange noises. Moaning like we were having a nightmare. My mom tried to move and scream, but it was like she had no voice. She remembered something her aunt told her. When evil spirits come to you, you are supposed to curse at them to make them go away. My mom started cursing at them and they immediately let get go. Right when they let her go, my dad and I stopped with noises. My mom fell asleep immediately after.

The next morning, we all went to my mom's aunt's house a few streets away. My mom told her experience to all her family. They all started to laugh when she was done. Right away my mom thought that they were the ones that were playing a joke on her. Then they started to tell her that her cousin's house was haunted and that no one ever wanted to go there. According to them, a curandera (witch doctor type) used to live at that house. When my mom's cousin was renovating their house, they found dolls and jars under the floorboards in the kitchen. Who knows what else that lady had done.

We learned that day that weird things would happen at that house. My mom's cousin would be walking down the hallway, and all of a sudden she felt someone push her from behind. Her arms felt like they were stuck at her sides and she couldn't put her arms out to catch herself. Needless to say, she easily broke her nose. She landed face first on the floor.

Another incident involved her little boy. He was sitting at the table eating breakfast with his mom and sisters. But he wasn't eating, he was just staring down the hallway toward his room. His mom would tell him to eat. It was like he didn't hear her. She finally yelled loud enough that he turned to her and acknowledged her. She asked what he was staring at. He said that his clown puppet in room was waving at him. It was like someone was holding it by the strings to make it wave at him.

My mom's uncle, who is a deeply religious man, saw something at that house. To this day, he will not tell anyone what it was that he saw. He said that he did not want to freak out anyone. We have a feeling that he saw the devil or something.

It was several years before my mom's cousin finally moved out of that house. But we never set foot in that house again.

Colonial Ghost
Bogota, DC Colombia

This story is about my first ghostly encounter (not that I've had that many, but being the first one I remember it as if it happened yesterday).

It happened when I was 10 years old. My uncle and his family were visiting Bogota for the first time in almost 6 years (they live in Houston). Because of this special occasion they threw a party for family and friends in the Sabana, the farming area outside the city (about an hour ride on car).

Joe Kwon's True Ghost Stories

This area is known for historical sites: beautiful old colonial mansions that are now hotels, restaurants or museums. We gathered in one huge mansion that was converted into a hostel. The afternoon went really well and we all had a great time.

By nightfall the adults got together in the meeting room to chat and relax. The owner of the hostel was renovating some of the areas and because the mansion was so old, he had to cut the electricity in the entire building. So we all had to rely on candles for light. Which meant that it was the perfect opportunity to explore the hostel.

So a group of 7 of us went to explore the upper floor but it wasn't very interesting. So we decided to head downstairs toward the basement. Most of the construction was taking place there.

When we got there it was pitch black. The candles were a little helpful, but for the most part we could only see the person that was a couple of feet in front of us.

One of my cousins started to tease us and joke about ghosts. He started touching us in the neck or blowing in our ears just to see who screamed the most. We were laughing quite hard until we started to hear some noises. At first they were a little faint, but they grew louder. They sounded like scratches in the wall. We thought it was my cousin, but he wasn't laughing, he got really quiet.

We continued on through this long hall and then I heard footsteps right behind me. One of my friends was walking next to me, and when we heard the footsteps we looked at each other thinking "did I just hear that?". I have to admit I started to get nervous and I can tell he was nervous too.

We kept walking and the footsteps grew louder, but this time we could tell it was the sound of somebody walking wearing boots. I didn't recall anybody in the group wearing boots, so my friend and I slowed down a bit and suddenly it got really cold around us, icy cold. The basement itself was below the ground but the temperature outside was rather nice as it was summertime, so we couldn't explain the sudden cold.

At that point my friend and I stopped walking. We were cold and frightened, we weren't sure what to expect next. So we didn't move and listened very carefully. The footsteps stopped just right behind us. And then we heard heavy breathing...I could feel the breath on my neck and I could even see my hair waiving a bit. And just like that my friend and I ran away as fast as we could!

When we got out of the basement we were going to yell at my cousin for the "bad joke". We honestly thought it was him following us trying to scare us.

But to our surprise he had already gone outside with the rest of the group. They all had been waiting outside for about a minute.

My friend and I still gave my cousin an earful for the prank, but he looked puzzled and swore that he wasn't the prankster. In fact, my friend and I were the last ones to come out of the basement.

We weren't sure exactly what had happened, but soon it was time to leave so we said our goodbyes and left the hostel.

A few months later my dad received in the mail one of the business magazines he was subscribed to. This particular edition had an article on haunted places in Bogota. I started to read it and came across a very familiar picture. I took me a few seconds to recognize it, but it was the same hostel we had gone to celebrate my uncle's visit. The article talked about how this mansion had been owned by a general back in the 1800's, back when the colonies were at war with the Spanish Crown for their independence. The general apparently was quite attached to the mansion and the surrounding area. After all, the property is simply beautiful and very peaceful: the mansion overlooking acres of gardens and pine trees. I don't blame him for trying to keep intruders away... It just so happen that on that particular evening, WE were the intruders.

My Cousin's Special Gift
Bogota, DC Colombia

My cousin has a special gift: she seems to be able to communicate with the deceased, but not by choice.

She has always been a very religious person, we are all Roman Catholic,

but she is particularly serious about it. She attends mass every Sunday, helps at the church often, participates in charity events, etc.

My grandfather died when she was 6 or 7. She was his favorite granddaughter, and she was quite devastated by his death. The day he died she "dreamt" that he was waiving goodbye from the sky. She got up from her bed and ran to the backyard and was crying hysterically when my grandma found her. She was pointing at the sky and my grandma saw a bright light behind a cloud, right where my cousin was pointing at. My cousin was yelling "Don't you see him grandma? He is right there!" My grandma saw the light vanishing in a matter of seconds; she tried comforting my cousin, and eventually she calmed down.

Two years ago, my mom was diagnosed with pulmonary emphysema. She couldn't breath well and had to carry a tank of oxygen with her all the time. In a matter of a few months her condition worsened, and one day my brother called me to say my mom was dying and we needed to get to the hospital soon. Sadly, as my sister and I were traveling down to Colombia, my mom passed away.

We arrived when my family was making all the arrangements for her funeral. My cousin came to the funeral home and stayed with me most of the time. Out of the blue, she told me that she had a dream the night before my mom's death. She said that in her dream, my cousin was going to a party and that in that party the only guests were family members that had passed away. My grandpa was there, my grandma (now deceased) was also there, a few more relatives that have died over the years, and my mom. She thought it was odd that my mom was there; she knew my mom was sick, but she wasn't dead. She told me that everyone at the party looked happy and my mom told her not to worry, that everyone was fine. She woke up from the dream at exactly 3 AM.

The next day (the day my mom passed away), my cousin was riding the bus to work and right around 1 PM, she felt slightly short of breath. Then gradually, she felt as if she was being asphyxiated. The feeling lasted about 10 seconds but it was quite unsettling.

As she was telling me all this, I remembered how my mom passed away, just as my brother told me. At around 1 PM my brothers and my dad were at the hospital with my mom. All of the sudden my mom started to feel out of breath, and in about 10 seconds she stopped breathing and passed away.

It was quite eerie so I asked her if she'd had any other similar experiences over the years. She said she had and when she dreams about deceased family members, she wakes up at 3 AM. It is known that paranormal activity peaks at 3AM!

I asked her to keep recording her dreams, but to this day I do believe this is a special gift.

Business Trip Encounter
Delhi, Delhi India

I was staying in Delhi for a few days during my business travels. I was traveling alone but was happy and I had a fantastic hotel suite that had great views of the city below.

After a busy day of meetings I arrived back at my room really exhausted, and I was also feeling a bit homesick, having been away from my family for two weeks and worried that they were all ok. So I took a hot bath and then snuggled up in bed to watch a film that was on tv about an expedition to Everest to take my mind off things. Then I gazed through my window at the people down below playing cricket. Soon I ran out of things to do so pulled on some clothes and decided to take a tour of the hotel.

The lobby was grand with a waterfall cascading into a pool and an inviting- looking cafe bar. I found that I felt a bit emotional, so I decided to take a stroll around their little arcade of gift shops for a bit of retail therapy! I bought a leather wallet for my husband in one shop and then tried on some pretty jewelry in another. I then came across a shop tucked away at the end of the row. I stepped inside and found an array of beautiful pashminas of all colors and patterns. The shop felt so inviting, and so I went in to take a better look. It appeared I was alone in the shop and so I decided to browse the shelves for something special for my mother.

I suddenly felt as if I was being watched, so I turned and saw a young Indian gentleman behind me who greeted me warmly and asked how he could assist me. I was a little surprised by his sudden arrival seemingly out of nowhere! I told him about my mission to find a gift and noticed he had the most beautiful friendly eyes. As he talked about the origins of the pashmina I had chosen, I felt as if I had known him forever. His mannerisms, his voice, his smile, and those eyes... all felt so familiar. It's hard to explain, but I felt calm and at ease, and almost trance-like.

He wrapped my gift in a delicate paper and passed it to me. I can't explain what happened next. He said in a soothing voice that he had made sure that my journey home would be free from problems, and I would arrive back home to find my family all safe and well too. But he said my worry today was valid, as my husband had been involved in a minor accident in work. But he said that he had been protected from injury and was just a little shaken up. You can imagine my shock and surprised! "Who is this!?", I thought. But there was something about him that made me feel a strong sense of trust in what he was telling me. He then gave me a warm smile and at that point it clicked. I did know him, I just wasn't sure how! And then gazed past me as if seeing someone else, so I followed his glance...

"Can I help you?" I turned to look at the man who had spoken, a large heavy-set man who had just stepped into the shop. Dropping my package to the floor I said "I was just buying... this man was just helping me..." but my voice trailed off when I turned to where my friend had been standing just seconds before. He was gone. I must have looked so very confused! The new shopkeeper looked at me as if I was mad! I explained his assistant had just been helping me out. To which he said he had no assistant. He worked alone.

I described my experience in so much detail because, although it is 6 years ago, I remember it all as vividly as it was yesterday. My encounter had a massive impact on me. I felt as if a protective veil had been placed on me after meeting my friend. I could not stop thinking about him, and wondering where I knew him from. He was so familiar. So you will probably want to know if he was correct about my husband and his accident... well I called him straight away and he did not mention anything. So I asked him about it. He was amazed how I knew about it! He said he was just bruised and had a lucky escape, and that someone must have been looking out for him that day! If only he knew...

Jay's Grave
Paignton, Devon England

I live in Devon, England. I own a car and me and a few friends regularly go for drives out on Dartmoor. We drive to places described in local legends and old folklore, such as the two bridges near Princetown and the residential home at Pixies Holt. Anyhow, we do this for fun normally or to laugh at who freaks out most. Google Dartmoor, England and it'll come up with a ton of ghost stories and local legends about the place.

This particular night we planned to stake out a place called Jay's Grave. She had died in the 18th century apparently, and has no known relatives or direct family. Basically no one cared much for her. This is what we got from the Internet anyways. The legend goes that she is buried in a roadside grave, and although she was a loner, fresh flowers will appear on her grave every night without fail marking her memory. On record, no one knows where these flowers come from or who placed them. So yeah, you

Joe Kwon's True Ghost Stories

can imagine why we staked it out, we were bored and curious on a Friday night.

For the record this happened on the 26 March 2010. We parked in a layby near the gravesite as due to the lanes near it we couldn't park any closer. We got out and sure enough there were flowers on the grave. This was about 9pm. We cleared the flowers from the grave and went back to my car. We had planned to stay there until morning.

We'd all just been sitting chatting and it got to about 3am. The lane outside was lit by the moonlight and we had a clear view of the grave so we could see anything. All of a sudden, three cloaked black figures walked past my car. We all saw it and just sat there in stunned silence, the leading figure was carrying flowers. A few of us freaked at this point, including me, but I didn't want to move, I was scared but intrigued at the same time.

Anyhow, my friend Lee, sitting in the front seat, opened the window and started shouting at these figures, just asking them if they were ok and stuff. They didn't acknowledge him. They stood motionless at the gravesite and then disappeared, just sort of faded away over the space of an hour.

I didn't drive off cause I was stunned, short of breath, almost. No one spoke for the entire hour this happened. We all agreed once the figures went, that we would stay until morning to see if there were fresh flowers on the grave.

Sure enough there was a fresh bunch there. We don't know what we saw but we all believe it is the funeral of

Mary Jay being repeated over and over every night because she has some unfinished business.

If you don't believe in Jay, just Google it on Dartmoor, or stake it out yourself...

The Hand in the Bath
Dublin, Ireland

Some friends of ours had recently moved to a new part of Dublin. The house they had bought was an old Victorian terrace that they fell in love with as soon as they saw it. It was spread over 3 floors with a spare bedroom and a large family bathroom on the top level.

The children especially loved the bathroom as it was huge and had a massive old roll to bath that they would fill and splash around in.

One night the youngest boy was washing upstairs in the old bathroom as usual when his mother who was down in the kitchen heard a terrible scream from him. She sprinted up the stairs to her son, fearing he had hit his head and was drowning, but when she burst in she found him cowering in the shallow end. He was sobbing and shaking and staring at the deep end where the plug was.

His mum pulled him out and asked him what was wrong. "Ma'am, I saw a hand under the water, it had been chopped off and blood was everywhere."

"Stop that Tommy," she said, "Stop being silly, there's no hand there. You scared me. You need a good night's sleep, and no more reading those ghost stories. They are making you see things! Now off to bed."

That night Tommy's mum filled up the bath for a nice long hot soak before she went to bed herself. The rest of the family was asleep and she was looking forward to relaxing with her book in the hot soapy water. As she lay there soaking, her foot moved and her toe touched something under the water. She looked up and saw a hand floating up towards her. She screamed and jumped out of the bath. She didn't even dry herself. Instead she got dressed, grabbed her family and fled the house with them. They went to stay with their Nan and Grandad in the country and never went back to the house in Cupcake Lane in Dublin ever, ever again.

The Other Side
Chalatenango, El Salvador

My house was located in a very little town named El Carrizal in the middle of nowhere. It was an hour away from the big city. Well, as I lived in that house I always had haunting experiences and bad souls or demons roaming around the house, but there was one thing that happened to me that was very disturbing to me.

I was around 7 to 8 years old. The heavy feeling that something was wrong had just begun. The air changed in a way that it gets thicker, and the gravity started to get heavier. I started to panic because I wasn't experienced enough to know what to do in a situation like that. Well, as I was lying in my bed I began looking around my dark room. I began to hear voices, but really far away like around where the kitchen was. They weren't speaking Spanish; I know that, but some weird language. I remembered that my grandma told me to always stay calm and confront what's there. I didn't, of course. I didn't know what she meant by that. But I did stay calm.

Seconds passed and they stopped talking. Then that's when I started to hear them as if they were walking around the house. It kinda felt like they were looking for something. That's when I noticed that I was only hearing the footsteps of one demon. What happened to other one???. I asked in my mind, of course. A couple of minutes passed, the noises had stopped, and all of the sudden I felt I was being watched. I ignored it, so I got up and started heading to the restroom.

I took my first step and I felt so dizzy and light-headed and really weak. So, I went in when I was washing my hands. I don't know if you've noticed, but you can still see your self in the mirror even if you looking down. So, yeah. I was washing my hands and the reflection wasn't doing what I was doing. So I looked straight at the mirror and my own reflection was already staring at me, kinda wit a smile on his face. I looked at it for a brief moment and ran to my room all freaked out.

Ever since that I hate mirrors, but now that I remember about it, my guess is that the other demon was in my room all the time just waiting for me to get up so then he can take over my body, but he couldn't because I'm too strong-minded for them. Its really hard to control a person if your strong minded. I'll explain a little more about the strong minded people and what it means actually in other of my stories.

DEATH
El Salvador

Everybody calls my Mini Hulk and almost all my friends know that for some reason I've always been haunted by some weird demon or ghost. To me it's not new, it's something that's been passed down from son to cousins and so on. Some members of my family have it, including my mom. She had never told me about this, but one day she confessed to me that she also used to see these things just like me.

Well, moving on to the story... (cause, I have so many, it's not just one, trust me!) I've been through a lot, especially if you live in EL SALVADOR.

It all started when I was 6 or 7 years old. I lived in a house that was built on top of a old cemetery that wasn't been used anymore. I always used to get up around 2-3 in the morning and stand in the corner of my room and stare at my room... ha-ha very funny... The thing is that it wasn't me, cause I sure don't remember doing this, but one day my grandmother started to sleep with me but in another bed that we had.

And yeah she knew about all this, she's like an expert at this stuff. But the moment she saw me she told me to wake up when ever you hear my whistle. And I was like huh? What are you talking about?

Later on it was like 9 p.m., everybody was going to sleep cause they get up early in the mornings. 12 something, pitch black, I got back up like sleep walking kind of, and to my right side I heard a whistle, very, very soft, but to my left side voices telling to come.

Luckily I remembered what my grandma said and I woke up... I was outside in the back yard. I turned around and my grandma was waiting for me at the door. And she said, "Thought you weren't gonna make it. And I was again like, "What? Why was I outside?" And she just told me just go to sleep and I'll watch over you ...so I did.

Three days later, it happened again, only this time I woke up in back yard where all the dead soldiers were buried... And trust me my house was big especially my back yard. My back yard was the cemetery. Just imagine how big that was.

Well I woke up, it was around 4 a.m. in the morning and my grandma just told me again, just follow my whistles if you don't want to end up going with Death. Cause supposedly it was Death after my soul.

So then night came again and this time my grandma actually got up like around 2 a.m. and went to that place where I woke up and did some sort of prayer chanting. And she told ha-ha your lucky it wasn't Death it was just a dead soldier [a demon] and just like that... and then she explained everything about ghosts, demons, and angels, and she told me that from this day on I will see all this weird stuff that I would be able to understand. She was right.

From that day on I've been dealing with the dead. Maybe this story is not that scary, but don't worry I've got plenty of stories to talk about, and how it gets worse. Even taking on a demon itself. My family's been doing it before I was born and now I carry the gift or curse.

The Shadow People
Tampere, Suomi Finland

I'm not really sure if this story could be classified as a ghost story or not. It is absolutely true. I'm not making any of this up.

I guess the story starts when I was born. I have one older sister by two years. Our family was completely normal. Married parents, both working and happy together. Apparently after I was born, my father literally changed over night. From loving family man he changed into aggressive and abusive. He started drinking heavily.

At the time we were living in a small house, and we had a ghost walking there in the night. She was an old woman. My mother was the only one that saw her. The ghost used to walk through one of the doors that we kept locked and sit at my mother's bed to wake her up, every time just before my father came home from the bar drunk. As I said, he was very abusive. It was like the ghost came to warn my mother so she could be prepared.

Anyhow, God knows why my mother stayed with my father. She did. We had a friendly family living next door and I used to play with the little boy a lot. Our parents got very friendly with each other as well. One day my friend's mother came over to talk to my mother and told her that my father came to their house the night before and was acting very weird. Apparently he sat at their kitchen table and started crying. Through his tears he said, "You have no idea how much blood there is... how horrible it is to chop someone into pieces and bury the body."

Now, this is something my mother told me only years later.

Anyhow, a few years went past. My father remained the abusive alcoholic he was. By the time I turned six we moved house. As soon as we moved, stranger things started happening. I started seeing these very scary creatures in our house. They were like human shadows, but instead of clinging to surfaces like shadows do, they were 3D. Like a human-shaped thing, but a shadow. You could see through them and they had no facial details or anything like that. They were always crouching, never standing. You could tell a lot from their body language. How they moved. They were fast. They never came too close to me. I could see them looking at me from the distance. I was terrified.

But it is strange how a small child's mind works. I got kind of used to them as I saw them so often. If I tried to get closer to them, they would run away from me. Like they were scared of me. They always ran into shadows and disappeared. Like under the table, or anywhere where there was a shadow.

I told my mother about them and I was so lucky to have a mother like her. She has seen a lot of really weird things in her life including having a poltergeist in her house when she was small. Anyway, my mother told me not to be frightened and to tell her every time I would see one. So I did.

All of a sudden my godfather, who was a close friend of my father, hung himself in a tree. Obviously he died. I stopped seeing these shadow people. My mother kept asking me if I saw any more and she came to the conclusion that they were foretelling my godfather's death.

Few months went past..... I started seeing them again.

I told my mother. She went nearly hysterical. "oh my God!! Who's dying now?"

I felt bad for upsetting her, so after that I didn't tell her much. Funny, how children sometimes feel so protective of their parents.

My grandmother (My father's mother) got really unwell. My mum just said, "Oh well, that's that then. She's gonna die." We were all expecting that. Until something REALLY weird happened.

I was going out to play in the park. We had this really long corridor you had to go through to get out. I got half way and I stopped. I saw one of those black shadow things crouching in front of me. It looked really aggressive. Like it was about to attack. I took one step closer to see whether it would get out of my way like they normally did. No, it wouldn't budge. It was swaying back and forth like it was just going to pounce on me, but I could see from the angle of it's head that it wasn't looking at me. It was looking in front of me.

I looked down just in front of me and there was another one, just like him, but it was white. It's hard to explain what a white shadow looks like, but just try to imagine it. It was crouching in front of me with its back facing me like it was protecting me. It also looked like it was about to attack.

So they did. They attacked each other and disappeared. After that my grandmother got out of the hospital and lived another ten years or so. And that was the end of me seeing these weird shadow creatures.

Also after that my parents got divorced. Thank God. Years later in my early twenties I went to see a hypnotherapist as I was suffering from panic attacks and depression. He took me back to my childhood memory that to him was the most important reason for my depression, and the memory was the first time I ever saw these shadow creatures. I really didn't remember how scared I was. It was near the long corridor in a shadowy corner and it was like one of those really terrifying nightmares where you're so frightened that you can't move or scream or anything. This shadow just stood crouching in front of me looking at me.

Story still goes on....

Years later when I turned thirty, I met my current partner. Now, his family also has had their fair share of strange things happening and due to these weird things, two of his cousins have become "psychic" sort of. Anyhow, they both have a "special friend" in the spirit world they can talk to. I guess kind of like a guardian angel. Apparently it is a network of all sort of spirits. Some good, some bad. Like humans.

It got me thinking. The white shadowy thing in front of me in the corridor... maybe I have a guardian angel. I asked my boyfriend if he could ask his cousin to ask her special spirit friend what the score is. So she did, and what she came back with I was not prepared for....

What the spirit said to her was that a long, long time ago my father obviously had done something really bad. There was a person who had put a curse upon our family. What that means is the person kind of summoned bad spirits to torment my father and completely ruin his life and tear the family apart. Which it did.

My father is in a bad state after drinking for thirty years. No one in my family is close really. I felt the need to move abroad, away from my family, and haven't spoken to my father for twenty years. Still, my sister has always been the one who tries to hold the family together somehow. She still sees my father and all.

Now, my boyfriend's cousin said that the curse is not strong anymore. It has done what it was set out to do. My father's life is ruined and the family is torn apart. The only person who is still apparently more affected is my sister.

She has been suffering from all sorts of strange illnesses for years. No doctor can find anything wrong with her. She has lost a lot of weight and is kind of an anxious person.

We have all discussed this and I am trying to find someone who can help to cleanse our family. Normally you would go to the person who put the curse on you, but apparently it was done so long ago that they're no longer alive.

As I said, all of this is true. It happened to my family. If you have any similar experiences, it would be nice to hear them.

Thanks for being patient. It is a long story.

The Evil Girl
Mayo, Europe Ireland

It was my birthday and to celebrate I went to Ireland. We went up the highest mountain and I slammed the car door shut and the sound kept repeating in my head. I told my brothers something's not right.

I heard a laugh. I swung my head round and saw a little girl around 8 years old. She just stood there laughing at me. But when I asked, "Who are you?" her facial expression changed. She frowned at me and said, "I have sinned, so have you... brother." Her eyes turned bloodshot and she walked off.

That night when I was in bed I felt something squeeze my hand. I shot up in bed. She held my hand tight until it was bleeding. She whispered, "Curse you, I will take you to hell with me."

I always see this girl in my head and hear the things she told me. Although it was 2 years ago I still remember like it's happening now.

Disturbing The Jinns
Islamabad, F82 Pakistan

When my sister moved from England to Pakistan for a long holiday in her new home, she shared a few stories of her time there. Everybody knows in Pakistan, even general Muslims know, that jinns exist. It's also mentioned in our holy Quran. In the villages in Pakistan stories are told quite often of 'no go' areas were jinns dwell. If you such as make this invisible being angry or even urinate on their tree (it is known for some jinns living in trees and have marked their own territory) it will possess you. So after hours it was advised by the very experienced and wise people to not to wander on your own.

Even my mum knew a few stories, but no one really knows what jinns look like. It's also believed that jinns have families and get married too. God created two worlds, one the seen, one of the unseen. They can even possess you and take all forms of shapes.

When I myself came to visit the village of Azad Kasmir

there was a relative of mine who became possessed by a jinn. He started talking and acting strange. The holy men were called in by his parents. They were frantic for their only son, and he was to marry soon. The holy man came and recited an exorcism prayer and ordered the jinn to speak. We learnt that the jinn was a female and said she loved the man and wouldn't leave his body. She had half paralyzed him and didn't want him to get married. She said, "he's mine, I'm not letting him go. I don't want him to marry. That's why I caused him to be disabled."

After a few sessions with the holy man, my cousin is now happily married and cured. But Pakistan, in the countryside with it being surrounded by hills, it was often told that deep in the mountains there were always drums being heard very late in the night. People knew it was jinns making those noises.

Coming back to my sister, her maid told her that her uncle in the village was viciously attacked by jinns or some other being. You have to understand the villages in the 1950s up to 1970s were very rural, with simple houses and homes. Most don't have proper toilets and some didn't have any at all. So people go to the forests to do their potty if you get what I mean. So, back to my story...

One evening her uncle went to do just that. As he went he was walking quite deep into the forest. He came across some noises, and as he looked on and slowly crept to see what was going on at this late hour, what he saw he will never forget for the rest of his life. There was a campfire and there were small people. Dwarf type, such as Rumpleskiltskin-type of characters. He was two feet, or maybe three-feet tall. He had pointy ears, pointing noise, devilish-looking jinns and women and children celebrating a wedding or some kind of event.

Her uncle at this point was quite scared and just after he was trying to make his way back he was discovered. They all just jumped on him, attacking him, ripping his clothes up. He just made it back alive. When he reached home everyone asked him what happened to him. He told them what had happened. They were all shocked.

Coming back to my sister again. My sister also had her elderly mother in law who was 98, however in good shape. She was also seeing things around her and in her bedroom. Being old it was said usually the very young or the very old could sense and see the unseen.

She complained of seeing such things around her constantly, but my sister couldn't see them. Some nights when my sister's mother in law would be poorly, she would sleep in the spare bed to keep an eye on her health during the night.

One night her mother in law was shouting and brushing herself off with her hands. Her hands seemed like they were hitting something. My sister asked her what's the matter. She said they are bothering me again. My sister asked who, and what do they look like? What are they doing?

She answered, "They're jinn people, they're running around me. They're very small and they jump on me. They are a nuisance." Only then did my sister realize it matched her maid's story, with the description of the tiny dwarf beings.

Since then my sister's mother-in-law has passed away and all her problems, too. But jinns do exist. I'm a firm believer.

I'm also very scared of these beings, but having said that, with strong belief and faith nothing could harm you. They say your night prayers keep the devils away...

Great Uncle George Comes to Play
Dunfermline, Fife Scotland

Great-Uncle George died at around age 6 of TB in Northern Ireland in the 1920s. I have two small sons, and as a medium, I know George comes to play here and at my mother's house in Edinburgh.

One night I was lying in bed with our new puppy, Roxy. She suddenly sat bolt upright and started growling at a spot near the window, her hackles raised.

NOTHING I could do, treats, toys, playing, would divert her attention. I could NOT settle her, and she had NEVER done this before.

I tried saying out loud the following: "George, I know you come to play and are happy here. I am happy to have you here. But right now our dog is scared and she might wake the boys up. Why don't you come back to play tomorrow instead?"

With that, Roxy gave a little sigh, turned round 3 times to make herself a comfortable spot, and went straight to sleep.

And of course he was back the next day!!

The Dirt Road
Evora, Foros Portugal

My grandfather told me this story about 10 years back or so when I was visiting.

It all happened one night when a friend of his drove past an uninhabited property using this dirt road as a short cut. His friend went into the woodland area about 20 minutes or so from the village close to this uninhabited property.

In the old days people used to live alone or as a family in properties throughout the woodland areas. Now in those areas it is completely dark at night except for the light reflecting from the moon. There would be no civilization for miles around.

His friend, whose name is Joao, drove past really late one night alone. As it's a dirt road, it's an uneven surface full of large holes so he had to drive quite slowly during this time.

He went past this old deserted property on the way to his end destination. The back of the house faces the road. He was calm, wasn't expecting anything to happen or to scare him. When he looked to his right he literally soiled himself.

He saw what looked like the figure of an old man standing motionless at the back of the old uninhabited house. The old man seemed to just be watching him. Joao didn't hang about to find out what he was doing there, or if he needed any kind of help, because he knew who he was. He put his foot down on the gas and sped up and never returned.

The last man who had lived there was my great grandfather, about 20 years ago. He died there. The man Joao saw was my great-grandfather. I was around 2 or 3 years of age at the time.

As far as I was told much, much later, my great-grandfather had a stroke or something and because he didn't want to be a burden to the rest of his family he committed suicide. It was sometime after he had that stroke, as he was unable to do much for himself after. He died on that property apparently in a great deal of pain. My grandfather, his son, found him lying on the floor.

To me, I love going down that road and stopping by his old place. I've never entered that house since just after his death when my grandparents were clearing out his things. But looking at that place, just being near it, even till this day, calms me down completely, gives me a sense of being watched over and I know by whom. I loved my great grandfather and always will.

I wouldn't be able to tell you now what his face looked like or his hair, what he wore etc. My memories are unclear and faded but I do know they were all good memories.

Death
Pretoria, Gauteng South Africa

I'm not sure whether it's ghosts but I can assure you it's quite scary.

Since I was small I used to have nightmares before someone died, but since the 8th grade in 2003 my "visions" took a different approach.

I was in a hostel and came home every weekend. At that time we found out that my step-grandad had cancer. One weekend in February 2003, I came home and my cousin visited me that Friday. At about 23:55 my parents woke up with a feeling of some kind of paranormal presence in their room. They went to sleep about five minutes later.

At that time I woke up and found myself lying on my back with my arms on my chest (I never sleep like that). I couldn't move. I was completely numb. I then felt someone sitting on my pillow. The funny thing is I wasn't the least bit afraid, until I felt it slowly moving away. When it was gone I felt afraid.

The next weekend the same thing happened, only it was on a Saturday night just before midnight.

Then the next weekend in the early morning of that Sunday, it happened for the last time. Three hours later my grandma phoned to say her husband was dead.

Then in May 2004, I can't remember the exact date, the same thing happened. That Sunday my other grandpa died.

Then on about the 24th of November 2006, I was packing my clothes because I was going to my aunt's house in Newcastle. Whilst packing I heard my mother calling me about three times, which was impossible as she wasn't home. It was actually more like screaming my name, a very urgent scream as if she was in danger.

Since that night I felt something was wrong and I couldn't shake the feeling.

When I was in Newcastle on about the 3rd of December, my cousin and I were alone at home, she was watching TV and I was playing on the computer.

I then heard another desperate, urgent call for me, I was really freaked out and scared.

Then on the 7th December 2006, my mother was almost hijacked and killed.

I know that this is a blessing, but it still frightens me alot, and I don't know who to talk to because I want to accept it but nobody I know could really understand or help me.

Demon Chasing Me in the Cemetery
Gothenburg, Sweden

10 years ago, me and my mates had a bet going on: the loser would have to walk through the cemetery in the middle of the night. The cemetery was huge and time-wise it took 15-20 minutes to walk through it (we clocked it during the daytime).

To make a long story short, I lost the bet and I was not very happy about it (I didn't show it of course).

I remember it was Saturday night and we had been partying hard. We had been drinking and I thought that this was the night to cross the cemetery.

The time was 0200 a.m. and we got the cab to the cemetery. I'll tell you that the cab driver was slightly concerned.

Once in the cemetery, we got out of the car and told the cab driver to wait for us.

Now I was standing outside the gate and looking into the dark and very old cemetery. I needed to light a cigarette and took my matches out to light it. The bet was to walk cross the cemetery and back and that would probably take me 20 minutes.

My cigarette was lighted and I took the first step into the unknown.

Volume 1 Ghost Stories from Around the World

The first 2 minutes were ok, because I still could see my friends, but they soon disappeared to small dots.

I was walking fast and the surrounding gave me a chill.

I managed to make it to the other side and now I had 10 minutes to go back. By this time I was so scared and started to see things. I knew it was my imagination playing a game, but it felt like 100 dead souls were watching me.

It didn't take long until I noticed footsteps behind me. I turned around and didn't see anything. I was freaked out and started to run. The scary thing was that the faster I ran the faster the steps behind me were getting. I was chased... I was in a panic mood and was running the fastest I could. The thing behind me was keeping up. I thought to myself that I cannot get caught here.

Then I saw my friends and even the cab driver smoking outside the cab. I was screaming and terrified. I almost could see their faces and also how they took off running. The cabdriver was fast, he left his car and he ran.

Now I was outside the cemetery screaming and the bloody sound was still chasing me. Then I suddenly stopped and so did the sound. I put my hands in my pocket and took the box of matches out and started to shake them. I started to laugh really hard. I was chased by the sound of my own matches.

Now I needed to find the cabdriver and my friends.

Someone in the Room
Cape Coast, Greater Accra Region Ghana

My wife and I are from Belgium. About four years ago we were doing volunteer work together at an orphanage in Ghana.

We had known each other for one year at that time. To celebrate our first year together while in Ghana, we went to Cape Coast. During this trip we had our first (and hopefully last) ghost experience.

Cape Coast is where a lot of the slaves were held before being transported to Europe and America. In this town stands the oldest European building outside of Europa: Elmina Castle.

A lot of African people died there during those days and the castle itself is quite creepy inside.

We stayed overnight in a small, dirty, but otherwise comfortable hotel close to the slave castle. I awoke around 6 AM with the feeling that someone else... a presence... was in the room with us.

I opened my eyes and was startled to see a black figure of a man standing behind the window curtain.

Before I had time to doubt what I was seeing, my wife suddenly woke up and asked, "Who is that man standing behind the curtain?"

Before we had much time to fully react, the figure vanished. The was no balcony... no place for a living person to escape to. The figure was there and then just disappeared right in front of both of us.

Blackness
Tenerife, Guia de isidora Spain

Two weeks ago boyfriend and I went on holiday to Tenerife, Spain. It was about 1:30 a.m. and we didn't know what to do. We're not the clubbing sort of people. We were

87

stuck for ideas for a while until I suggested to drive up to the mountains above the clouds.

My boyfriend loves stars and things to do with astrology. That's why I suggested that. It was absolutely pitch black driving up the mountain roads and not another car in site.

After about half hour of driving he stopped at a view point. Complete blackness surrounded us cause there were no street lights. One exception though, if you looked up, there was this not very well lit up house. But it was inhabited, least I think it was as it looked modern.

There weren't any stairs to get down to where we were, not that I could see anyway, and it was easily a 100 feet drop. But that was the only civilization I could see for miles around.

Anyway both of us got out of the car. Immediately I felt weird, as if I couldn't breath well. I looked all around me, but nothing but the blackness surrounding me.

My boyfriend was happily staring up at all the stars, but I couldn't stay outside any longer. I just wanted to leave this place. So after a few minutes

I ran back into the car where I felt I could slightly breathe.

During the process of being outside those few minutes I did take a few pictures of the towns below us and of my surroundings. When I looked back at one of my photos I could clearly see a figure, a face of some sort. There were what looked like orbs. Most were just dust particles stuck to the camera lens, but one clearly wasn't. It was a face, with its mouth wide open as if screaming out something.

I was glad to just get out of that place when he finally got back in the car and drove. By the little religious statues there and the flowers, I'm assuming someone died there in the past.

Don't think I'll be doing any midnight drives on that road ever again.

Pig
Catocna, Gutiapa Guatemala

I do tend to believe in Ghosts; and such, and I have encountered small spirits in my life. But what I would have never actually imagined was that my own father had also encountered something, and it was when he was a young boy.

In 1975: In the Country of Guatemala; my father and his family lived in a small city. My father, as a young boy, had many friends. Most of which would be reckless and troublesome. But when they found out about the "Pig Woman" as little kids, they didn't believe.

An old woman lived in a quiet part of the city. Like any neighborhood, kids played outside and enjoyed themselves. Children didn't know much about this woman, as she kept to herself. Later would they find out, that she (or what they would tend to call her) was a witch.

My father, as a boy, remembers one day that him and his friends were playing outside near the old woman's home. A pig was spotted staring at them from the bushes. Earl, a brother of my father, noticed it. He and the rest of the little boy group started to terrorize the poor pig. They started to beat up the pig, leaving it all cut up and wounded with blood. My father even remembers Earl had grabbed out his pocket knife (in this part of the city, you would always need to carry one) and cut the pig with an "L" shaped cut below its head. After beating up the pig, they had left it to die on the side pavement of the road. They had planned to want to finish off the pig, but they didn't bother to do anything to it anymore.

To this day, I'm glad my father didn't get involved with this animal abuse.

The next day my father was terrified. The old woman had been spotted, and she was all bruised up. Cuts on her arm, leg, and face. My father's brother did not believe that it was the same doing of the pig, that was until they noticed a "L" shaped cut mark on the old woman's throat. That's when he got scared.

Many people after that believed she was a witch and able to transform into the form of a pig.

Even now, years afterwards, my father believes that his brother was cursed from that old woman. Earl had many mishaps in his life: his wife lost their baby, he lost his home, and the actual part that scared him the most is that some nights, he'd actually dream of the pig- to see it transform back into the old woman, to then beat him up and cut him up with the same "L" cut under his throat.

Luckily, my father NEVER took part in this, nor will he ever. Just remembering this always scares him and worries him that the old woman will appear in his dreams. "That old lady is probably still alive today, kept up in that small house of hers. Just waiting to transform herself into another form, and see who mistreats her; so she can place a curse on them. It sends chills down my spine just thinking that there ARE things in this world that are just so hard to believe."

Knock Knock Knock . . .
Fareham, Hampshire England

This story is true. Every letter - every sentence is exactly how it happened. I wouldn't be wasting my time making this up. I'm not that type. All I want to do is share my experience with others who know how it feels. I just wanted to make that clear before I began.

This true story happened at my Grandma and Grandad's new house. They invited us round for dinner.

It was about 4:30 when we first got a glimpse of the house. Who I mean by we - Me, my sister (Hannah) and my Mum. We were driving through a deserted countryside when we saw it. I will always remember that house. A very old house with moss creeping up the sides of the house. A thick wooden door with a golden gargoyle door knocker. It looked entirely out of place here in the sunny countryside.

We pulled up on the concrete drive. I stepped out and saw the house up close. It looked terrifying. Old, big and ugly. Ewwwww!

We were ushered in the house by my eager Grandparents. It looked different inside. Clean, spacious, modern. Strange!

We sat down at the dinner table, wolfing down a delicious roast dinner with champagne. I was only 17, and my Mum said I was too young for champagne. I felt like the odd one out.

Just then, I heard a knock at the door. I was the only one who heard it. Very weird. I told my Grandparents, but they were too deep in conversation with my Mum and told me to answer. Maybe that was why they couldn't hear it. Maybe...

I walked to the door. I never liked opening the front door at night and today was no exception. My hand leant down to the doorknob, but leapt back again. It was steaming hot! My Grandad said 'Well are you going to answer it or not?' and laughed. Mum and Hannah joined in. I scowled. They didn't know!

So I covered my hand with my sleeve and opened the door. No one was there. I frowned. Weird.

As soon as I shut the door I heard giggling. Kids! Probably just a game of knock door run!

Volume 1 Ghost Stories from Around the World

I sighed as I walked back to the dinner table. 'Well who was it?' my Grandad asked. 'A game of knock door run' was my reply. Grandad tutted. "Great way to treat new neighbors!" he laughed.

But then I thought about it. There weren't any neighbors. We are completely alone in this countryside. How could – Knock, Knock, Knock!

I jumped. My Grandad rushed to the door. He pressed his ear to the wood. He said he heard giggling. He put his hand to the doorknob. He jumped away and swore. ' What is it Dad?' My mum asked.

' The doorknob.' He said. 'Its freezing!'

My heart thumped. When I touched it, it was hot. But when my Grandad touched it, it was freezing. Crazy!

Grandad then rushed to the door and opened it using a kitchen towel. The bushes outside rustled as the sound of giggling and footsteps were all to be heard. My Grandad shut the door' 'Bloody kids!' he shouted. Suddenly the laughing stopped. It was weird. Just after he said it - nothing.

Knock-Knock-Knock.

This time it was slower and heavier. The hairs on the back of my neck stood up.

My Grandad grabbed a baseball bat - he loved baseball - and marched to the door. First he put his hand on the door knob. Not hot or cold. Normal. Then he pressed his ear to the wood. We all did the same.

Then a voice spoke up. This voice has stayed in my mind ever since this day. It was low and unsteady, but sounded like it came from a young boy. It said:

'Now you've made me angry. Send death my regards.'

I screamed, my Mum screamed, my sister screamed, my Grandma wheezed. My Grandad, on the other hand, slammed open the door, shook his baseball bat and yelled 'That's enough! Now come out this instant and I'll show you-'

He stopped. There was no - one there.

After a few hours of sitting down by the fire calming down, I went to the toilet. Mum protested, she said she wanted us to stick together. I said I really needed to go and she reluctantly let me. I shut the bathroom door, locked it, and took a tinkle.

That voice was drifting in my mind and I got kind of scared. I flushed the chain and quickly washed my hands. I quickly looked up into the mirror above the sink and froze.

Behind me was a boy. Pale skin, ragged clothes, scruffy hair. Looked about seven or eight. He was mumbling something in a very strange language, but all the time is big, round black eyes were focused on ME. I feel ashamed saying this, but I'm sure you would understand, but I actually almost fainted. I was terrified.

I decided it was best to run out and lock the door, trapping this young boy, but I didn't want to make any sudden movements. I didn't know what it would do. So - very slowly - I slid closer to the door, my eyes never leaving his. He was still muttering something in a weird language. Very slowly, my hand reached out to the door on my right. My fingers touched the doorknob. I was about to leg it but I stopped dead in my tracks. His hand reached out and squeezed my arm, making it impossible to move it. His hand was so cold and so strong. I almost crapped my pants.

I closed my eyes, unsure about what to do, hoping Mum would walk in, wondering where I was. Just then, the hand moved away. I opened my eyes, and the boy was gone.

I ran out the bathroom. One thing I found strange was that the bathroom door wasn't locked. I swear I locked it when I walked in.

I ran to my Mum and told her we needed to get out. I also told her Grandma and Grandad weren't safe in the house. They said that I was just a little bit spooked and they insisted on staying.

A few hours later, we were back at my place. My mum phone Grandad to check they were fine, just like I told her to. They were fine.

I was beginning to move on with my life. My little incident at the house was 8 months ago. I forgot all about it.

One day, I was walking home from school with my beautiful girlfriend, Ruby. We were the only ones in the house so we decided to have a little fun. We were stopped halfway into our lovemaking session when the phone rang. I reluctantly ran downstairs to answer it, putting on my pants as I ran. I picked up the phone and pressed it against my ear. I froze when I heard a voice at the other end of the line. IT WAS THE SAME VOICE AS THE ONE I HEARD AT MY GRANDPARENTS' HOUSE!

I was so scared. It was muttering that strange language just like it was in the bathroom 8 months ago. I mustered up all the courage I could find and said shakily, ' Wh-o a-re yo-u?'

It giggled. It was the same giggle as well! Then it hung up.

I was just an ordinary boy before these events took place. You probably won't believe it. I wouldn't believe it if I hadn't lived through it. But, ever since these events took place I have been haunted by this boy. I have nightmares. I can't sleep. I keep imagining the boy wherever I look.

I am now a 29-year-old man.

Meeting the Man with No Face
LaPorte, Indiana USA

Growing up, I loved to listen to my family sit around the kitchen table and spin stories of the weird and unexplained that they had experienced in their lives.

The stories that always caught my attention were the

accounts that many people in my family had with the man with no face.

The way they would describe him was that he was a tall man, dressed from head to toe in pitch black clothes and there was nothing but a black void where his face would be.

Over the years, I would dive deep into the world of the paranormal. I came across stories with almost the same type of person being run over by a car, but upon further inspection, there was no one there and no damage to the car. (This is what my mother and sister swear happened to them.)

November of 2001 was my turn to meet this strange man that had haunted my family for years.

I was working as a desk clerk in New Buffalo, Michigan. At the end of my shift I walked out to my car and couldn't help but feel like someone, somewhere was watching my every move. I thought nothing of it as all I wanted to do was go home and get some rest after a busy day.

It was 11:00 p.m. when I drove up to the main intersection in town. Everything in town is closed by at least 9 or 10 PM. So, nobody was around as far as the eye could see. But something caught my attention and put fear into my heart.

Sitting on a bench in front of the local drug store was a man, dressed from head to toe in black. He had his hands on his lap and his head hung down with a hood covering it. I had to stop for the red light and in the back of my mind I could hear my consciousness screaming, "Don't look at him! If you look, he's going to get you!"

I sat there waiting for the light to change, never once looking at the man except out of the corner of my eye. He never moved. Not once.

As the light turned green, I dared to look in his direction, and he stood up and came walking towards my car at a very fast pace, pulling back his hood to show me that there was nothing but a black void where his face would be. I laid on the gas and drove off as fast as I could. Looking in the rear view mirror, I saw him stop and stand where my car had been, watching me as I drove away.

I came home and told my sister what had happened, and she could only smile and ask how a grown man, who could read stories of ghosts and hauntings and demons, could be so scared.

Let me tell you; there is a major difference between reading the story and BEING the story.

I have had many more run-ins with the paranormal over the years and will be more than happy to post them here for your reading pleasure.

The Mysterious Giggles
Pandan Indah, Kuala Lumpur Malaysia

Now this story happened to a room-mate of mine when I

was in college years ago. I was living in a hostel of 13 stories, called Maxis Tower, with my room being on the 10th floor. From what I was told, this tower used to be a commercial building before it was converted into a dormitory, why I'm not sure. On each floor there's a huge middle area which is the general lounge with 4 big rooms that contains 10 students (all girls since this is the girl's dorm) situated opposite each other. So there's about 40 students and we pretty much knew each other well enough. Now, in the middle of the big lounge is a big concrete pole where they plug all the appliances like tvs, radios etc. This pole only exists from my level to the 13th floor (I know, odd architecture huh). Anyway we shared the same general bathroom and toilets all in one huge ladies room. Rows of toilets and shower stalls face each other in there.

One night, my roommate came back from an outing with a few of her friends. It was a little past midnight I think so my roommate and her friends were eager to get cleaned up and rest. She got the other girls to go shower at the same time since we're all chickens when it comes to going to the bathroom at night and for good reasons too. I think there were 5 of them attacked the shower stalls all at once lol. Other then that, from what they claimed, there was nobody else there. Note that these shower stalls have numbers on them, with the doors slightly raised from the floor so that you can see if it's vacant or not. The girls chatted to each other cheerily while showering. Then they heard giggling out of the ordinary since none of them could point out which of the girls were laughing plus the conversation was not that funny! Then they heard this 'girl' started saying "satu, ada...dua, tak ade..tiga ada!" and so on which translates to 'her' peeking at the shower stalls and counting mischievously and playfully saying, "Stall 1 occupied. Stall 2, vacant. Stall 3 occupied!"

By now all the girls stopped their chit-chats and quieted down trying to figure out who was saying that. Then the 'mystery girl' did the most eerie, but still playful giggle again. In the middle of her giggling, my room-mate got curious and rushed out of her shower stall in a split second just to catch who was it that thought it was funny -- interrupting them like that only to find no one outside the stalls! The toilets were all empty, too. As I said, you could easily know since it's built in opposites. There was no way the 'girl' could have run off that quickly without any footsteps heard.

Another girl came out of the shower as well asking my roommate who was it and all she got was her pale face. She understood it instantly, and feeling spooked she quickly rushed the other girls to finish up. The others didn't really ask why, but they obliged. They quickly got out of the showers, and marched right into my room along with my roommate since our room was the closest to the shared ladies room.

Me and the other girls remembered being surprised at seeing all 5 girls in towels still dripping wet and pale-faced as they entered the room. Without wasting any time they told us of what happened and got us all thinking. It might just be one of the girls trying to pull a prank on them but I personally doubt it. When you live together like us and away from home in a strange place like that, the last thing you want to do is to creep each other out! Plus nobody could point out whose voice it was which is very easily done since we all were quite close.

By the way, there have been sightings of a mysterious looking girl always close to the giant concrete pole especially at night, when the TVs are out and as usual nobody bothered to ask who she was but always failed to find out about 'her' later. We decided to keep quiet of the matter since we didn't want to spook the rest of the girls too. We've even had girls complaining that someone was always naughtily knocking on toilet doors and everything seems to happen randomly. Shrugs.

She Scared Me But I Forgave Her
Glasgow, Lanarkshire Scotland

This one happened around three and a half years ago when I was at Reid Kerr College.

I never liked the feeling I got in any part of that building, it always made me tense up with fear and it just wasn't nice. Mostly though the worst feelings you got happened in the girls toilets, they were always very cold and I often heard whispers, sometimes saying my name and others were to quiet to make out.

One time we heard a voice and were in a different room than it. As soon as I stepped into the room I wanted to get back out again. It was depressing, suffocating and too loud (only to me). Half way through the lesson, I turned to my friend Kevin and said, "I feel like someone has hung themselves in here." He just stared at me and I began to feel even more uneasy.

Again back to the girls toilets, I was standing in front of the mirror (for longer than I usually do because I don't like mirrors) and then my eyes traveled to the left. Behind me there was a girl standing staring! I turned around and she was gone.

I ran out crying and only told Kevin what I'd saw.

Also in this toilet there was a wheel chair, it was always folded away during the day but at night, it was sat in the centre of the toilet, in front of the mirror. I thought nothing of it, as I knew someone would probably just be messing about with it.

One day though I never really noticed it in the middle of the room as I went to wash my hands. When I finished and went to walk out the door, I tripped over the wheelchair and it didn't move. I got the feeling someone was sitting in it and ran out the door. A day later a huge bruise appeared where I banged my ankle on the wheelchair. That wasn't right.

A few weeks later we had a movement class but none of the girls were changed for it. Our tutor asked why? And one of the girls said, "It's too cold in the girls toilet and it creeps me out." Our tutor replied, "That's because there's the ghost of a girl in there". The girl thought he was having a joke but he said he wasn't joking.

On the last days of college, I decided to tell the class my experiences and one of them said I should speak to the receptionist as she knows the story of the building.

Turns out that a girl hung herself there, for she had fallen in love.

After hearing this I felt really sad for her as she was only young and now was trapped there. I kinda didn't fear her anymore and felt a bit better that I knew, she meant no harm.

This is one of my saddest ghost experiences.

The Lakes
Cumbra, Langdell Cumbria

Two years ago I was swimming in Fell Lake and as I swam I felt someone pulling my arm to stop me. As I slowed down I saw a young girl beside me. "Hello." She just looked at me, then she pointed with her head, as if to say look where you are going.

So I stopped and turned to her but she had gone. I looked around but no one was there. So I swam back to the bank where my friends were.

On my return the same girl was standing there (like she was waiting for me). As I approached her she disappeared in front of me. I thought I drank too much lake water.

Over then next 5 weeks I swam there every time I got to that point the girl was there.

It was when I met up with my frends I told them and my friend's mum told me that the girl was Sofia, who drowned in the middle of the lake. At the same point where I saw her. Still to this day I meet her. The lake has an undercurrent and she stops anyone from drowning.

Mountain Man
Beirut, Lebanon

When I was about 8, my two older brothers, my cousin, and I drove to a mountain to spend the day there. We got there and got out of the car and hiked up the mountainside. We came to a small cave and went inside. We sat there and ate, then relaxed for about twenty minutes.

Then my oldest brother said something that I didn't believe at first. He told us a story about how an old guy used to live in a cabin, about 50 years ago, on this mountain somewhere. He said that the guy was weird, mentally insane, and one day a couple of hikers came across his cabin and he came out with his knife and tried to kill them. They got away and came back with the police. He came out again at them and the police shot him. His body fell down the mountain and they were never able to find it again, but he still haunted the mountain.

When my brother was done we all laughed because we didn't believe him. We walked out of the cave and continued our hike. Later on in the day we were walking and rocks started falling next to us. We looked up and saw rocks sliding down the mountain. We ran and got out of the way.

Then we heard something that still scares me till today, we heard a man shrieking. Then we saw him running across the mountainside. He looked like he was wearing a red shirt, then I realized that he was covered in blood. My brothers and cousin ran, but I couldn't move. I was frozen in fear, as I watched the man ran straight for me with something in his hand, but my brother came back grabbed me and we ran.

When we looked back he was gone. We ran to the car and drove away. Now I believed that the story my brother told us was true. We never went back to that mountain and never told anyone about what happened up there.

The Wee Laddie
Edinburgh, Lothian Scotland

To this day I still maintain that I have never encountered a ghost. I need to maintain that belief because otherwise I would go insane. I really do not want to see ghosts and get all freaked out, who does? What happened to me back in the early 90's must have a very simple explanation and back then it was discussed with family and friends, then re-discussed until I was told to forget it and move on. Anyway, here goes.

I install, service, repair and maintain gas central heating systems in and around the Edinburgh, Lothians and Fife area of Scotland. I arrived at a house in the heart of the city to carry out a service on a heating boiler. The woman, I remember, was very pleasant, very chatty, and offered me a cup of tea before starting the job. She then took me to the boiler that was in a cellar down some stairs at the back of the property. She said she'd leave me to it and then left.

I went about my business, the usual service routine. I was about 5 minutes into the job when this boy appeared. A very real boy. I can't remember the exact conversation word for word, but it was something like this, "Hiya, what ye doing, Mister?" I got a bit of a start, but said, "Hi there, just cleaning out the boiler." And I do remember asking him why he wasn't at school. He told me he wasn't feeling well and he was allowed to stay off. He said he might go fishing in the afternoon. I asked him if fishing makes him feel better and he said that he feels ok. I turned and looked at him. He was about 8 years old, and I said with a hint of laughter, "But you just said you weren't feeling well and that's why you are off school." He said, "Yeah, I lied to my mum, I really want to go fishing."

I found it amusing and carried on with the job. There was no more conversation after that and I had the Hoover on almost continuously so I couldn't hear any anything anyway.

When I was done, I called upstairs to the woman to come down and see the finished job, all clean and tidy. She was delighted and we walked back up the stairs. As she began to lock the door I said to her to make sure her son wasn't still in there. She looked at me and said, "What? I haven't got a son, I haven't got any children." I explained to her what had happened. I felt like an idiot because she was looking at me as if I was a lunatic now. I must have had a slight desperation in my voice because I was asking about neighbor's children, could it have been one of them who jumped the garden wall and came into the cellar.

The woman turned slightly weird when I think back, but then confirmed that on two other occasions, workmen have encountered the boy. She herself had done some research on the house and the area in news articles, and one story that she did find was that a boy did live in the house in the early 20th century and drowned in the "water of Leith." The story did not confirm that the boy had been fishing. The woman herself had never encountered the boy, only (including me) three workmen.

To this day I like to think it was a neighbor's son playing truant from school. In fact I've convinced myself of that. It certainly freaked me out for months, boilers in basements were a no go area for a while!

Man with a Lantern
Co, Louth Ireland

It was 10.00 p.m. on July 5, 2008. I was sitting in the sunroom with my dog Dillon beside me. I was reading a book, when all of a sudden he started to bark.

I said be quiet, but he did not stop, and then all of a sudden he got up and ran to the door. (Our door was half glass so you could see right through the window.)

When I looked up, I saw this man dressed in around 1900 clothes, and he held a lantern. I froze and closed my eyes, and when I opened them it was gone.

I ran to my mum and told her what had happened. She said it was my eyes playing tricks. But, I don't think so because what is so weird is my dog started to bark at it. I have never seen one again.

Imaginary Friend
Bedfordshire, Luton England

When I was little, like a lot of other children I had an imaginary friend. I don't remember her ever speaking to me and I never knew her name.

She wasn't with me constantly, she would come and go as she pleased and I would usually only see her in my house. She wouldn't follow me to school or anything.

It used to drive my mum and dad mad. I'd sit in my room all day talking to and playing with my friend.

I used to collect these little animals called 'Puppy in My Pocket' and my collection grew to include other animals like cats, rabbits and horses etc.

One day my imaginary friend and I were playing with my little toy animals whilst my sister, with whom I shared a room, watched from the bunk bed.

Suddenly my sister started screaming and ran downstairs. I didn't really know what to make of it and just carried on playing.

Later in the day my mum and dad called me downstairs and asked me who I was playing with and if course I answered 'my friend.' Then they asked me what she looked like and I replied 'she looks just like me.'

Soon after that day I didn't see my friend anymore.

A few years ago my family and I were talking about that day and my mum asked me if I remembered. I said that I did but that I didn't really understand what happened.

They told me that my sister had started screaming that day because she could see I was playing with one of the toy dogs but she could also see another one that I wasn't touching moving too.

She ran and told my parents what had happened.

When I said my friend looked like me it really scared them because a few months into my mum's pregnancy with me she had a partial miscarriage, it turned out she was supposed to have twins.

Make of this story what you will, but my family and I believe that it wasn't an "imaginary friend," but my twin.

Joe Kwon's True Ghost Stories

Hard Worker
Manila, Philippines

The names I used in here are not their real names.

This happened back when I was in the Philippines over 5 years ago. I used to worked as a receptionist at one of the famous but very old hotels in Manila. My days of working there were fine. I met Christy (not her real name). She is a very kind and helpful person. She made everything so easy for me when I was in training.

We became really good friends. She would tell everything but her past. When I tried to ask her about her past life or when she was a kid, she would say, "It's not very exciting," and she would change the subject right away. But it just made me so curious. It made me felt like she was hiding something from me...

One day at work, she was so weird. She looked very pale and it seemed like she was so scared. I talked to her and told her to take a day off and rest since she doesn't looked very good.

Suddenly she looked at me like I said something very hurtful and she looked like she might hurt me. I got scared a little, not because she might hurt me but because there might be something wrong with her. I have never seen her like that angry for almost one year of working with her before.

Then she suddenly left.

The next day, she was herself again. She was so happy that day that she even invited me and our two other co-workers over to her house for a dinner. She didn't mentioned about yesterday. I couldn't ask her about it cause I didn't want to spoil her mood.

So me and my other two co-workers decided to just drive my car. I have never been to Christy's house before. But her house is not that hard to find.

While in the car, my co-worker Angie asked me, "What happened to Christy yesterday?" She said, "She looked like she was on drugs." And my other co-worker Melba asked, "Are you guys got into a fight or what?"

I didn't know what to say since I didn't know what really happened to her.

So we got to her house. It was an old house, but I'm not sure how old it is.

We knocked 4 or 5 times but nobody answered. So I called her phone. She answered it but in a weird voice, I almost didn't believe it was her. She said to just come in, but I said the door is locked. She said to come in and she hung up the phone. So I told my other co-worker to just come in. They looked at me for a minute and tried opening the door. It was locked. So we were annoyed. My two co-worker said to just forget about it and go home when the door opened.

Cristy opened it. She said that she left the door opened for us cause she was busy cooking.

It was a very good dinner. After dinner, we drank wine while watching movies. Then I felt a need to go to the restroom, so I asked her where is her restroom. She told me where it was, so I went and found it. When I was doing my business, the light suddenly flickered. I didn't think anything unusual about it, it might be because the house was old, I thought.

When I was finishing up and about to wash my hands, there was no water coming out. I was a little frustrated and about to go out of the restroom when the water started running. I swear to God I had turned the handle to off and no water should be coming out. A little freaked out, but I went ahead and wash my hands anyway. Then the water suddenly turned brownish. And it smelled really bad. I was so shocked and disgusted. I turned off the water and went running to the living room and told the guys what happened. They looked at my hands, and smelled them, they said it smelled like soap. I couldn't believe it, but when I smelled it, yes it smelled like soap. I tried to convince myself that I was just imagining things, maybe I drank too much wine.

Finally we decided to call it a night and drive home. When I got home after dropping off my co-workers, my room mate who was also my cousin, said, "Oh my God! Did you go swimming in the sewers? You smell so bad!" she said this while holding her breath, and when she couldn't hold it she threw up. Now I knew I was not imagining things.

After 3 hours of cleaning myself, I decided to go to bed since I was so tired.

The next day at work, my two co-worker Angie and Melba called in sick. I was worried, so I planned on visiting them after work.

Melba and Angie looked horrible, I couldn't believe how they lost so much weight in one day. They were so skinny and they looked 30 years older than they were. I tried to talk to Angie since Melba was sleeping. I asked her what happened to them, and she just kept on saying, "It hurt, please help us, it hurt so bad," that's all she could say. I felt really bad for them, and I suddenly felt that I needed to do something.

I called Christy, and asked her to meet me at the coffee shop we always hang out. She said yes.

We were quiet for a minute, then I told her what happened to Angie and Melba. She looked at me for a second then said, "It's her again," in a very low voice. I said "who?" She didn't answer. I got really frustrated when she did this. I asked her again, this time with an angry voice I couldn't control. So she looked up, and said I would not understand. I said I promise I will try to understand. So began her story...

First of all she had an identical twin sister. They were both at the age of 12. Her twin sister's name was Anne. Anne was so different from her, even though they looked the same just like if you look in the mirror. Anne was very violent when she did not like things. She got really jealous towards Christy. She used to sneak up to Christy's room and steal her favorite dolls and buried them in their yard. Christy caught her one night digging outside with her stuff, ready to be buried. She was so mad and went to her sister. They got into a fight and she accidentally killed Anne. She didn't want anybody to find out about it, so she buried her where Anne had been digging.

Their parents went looking for her sister, but they couldn't find her. After a time their parents just gave up.

Since then Christy's been having nightmares about Anne. And she's started hearing voices in her room. It still happens till now she said. Cristy tried to say sorry to Anne and tried to explain, but Anne would just laugh at her. When we were at her house for a dinner, Christy said she was there the whole time watching us, and that she was angry. After we went home, Anne said that she's not gonna have friends for too long. Cristy was so mad, but before she could say anything, Anne was gone.

After hearing this, I didn't know what to say. I couldn't find any words to start with. I had mixed feelings...

I will have to post what happened next since this is already too long. This is true. That's all I can say.

Third Day
Quezon City, Manila Philippines

My cousin studied medicine. She is a doctor by profession. She also has the ability to see and experience paranormal entities. She is 16 years older than me, but we are close. She often tells us stories of ghosts in the hospital, especially the morgue. One thing she told us is that, on the third day, on the exact 72 hours after a person's death, you can see a smoke coming out of the body and that it would last a couple or more seconds.

I haven't really experienced that until my dad died. I was at his wake and was busy talking to my friend, when I felt someone brush my hair. It was like someone saying hello or something. I thought someone just arrived and wanted to talk to me so looked back. No one was there. I looked back at my friend. She was pale and couldn't speak. I asked her why, she said she saw a dark figure behind me touch my hair.

I joked and said, maybe it's my dad saying take care, like he always does. I meant it as a joke, but when I looked at my watch I realized it was my dad's third day. I hurriedly went to see my cousin and she confirmed it.

Strange Child
Dolores, Michocan Mexico

When I was about eleven years old I went to Mexico to

visit my father. One night my aunt took me to my other aunt's house. I stayed there for the night and slept in her little boy's room. Outside of the window was a light and I asked her to leave it on because I was scared of the dark. I fell asleep and began to have a weird dream.

In my dream, a little girl in a pink dress with a black collar walked in.

She seemed friendly, but then I saw her hands. She had long, thin fingers and she began to grab my hand. She was trying to tug me under the bed. I tried to scream and wake up, but the little girl in my dream wouldn't let me. Finally I woke up, but right before I did she let go of my hand and scratched me with her nails. When I woke up I realized I had been sleeping and it was just a dream. Until I looked down and saw I had a scratch on my hand with a little blood

I looked around to see if I could have done it with something, but there was nothing I could have cut myself with. Then the next day I told my aunt what happened. She told me that when they first were building the house they used to see a little girl in the shadows. What I thought at first was just a dream, I now know was real. That little girl was trying to hurt me.

My aunt's kid is a little boy and he is the only child in the house, but nothing ever happens to him. But when young girls stay there, things always seem to happen to them.

The New Car
Loanhead, Midlothian Scotland

Back in '97 I bought a new car. The day I went to pick it up, my 3 year old daughter cried to come with me. I said ok and I took the child's car seat with me.

We eventually got to the place and did all the paperwork, etc, and finally got the keys and were shown to the car. The salesman said his goodbyes and left. I spent 5 minutes fixing the child seat onto the back seat and then strapped my daughter in to her seat. Even at 3 years old, she knew it was a new car and was excited. And off we went. We laughed and sang Disney songs on the way home. Was great.

That night the whole family were at the dining table eating our evening meal. So it was my wife, two sons and my daughter. All were talking about the new car. My eldest son asked my daughter if the car was good. My daughter replied with laughter, "Me and daddy and the man sung songs."

"What man?" everyone asked.

"The man sitting beside daddy in the front, he was funny."

I went cold. I took her out to the car and asked her to show me where the man was sitting. She pointed to the front passenger seat. I figured this was too heavy a thing for a 3 year old to say. Why would she make something like that up too? She saw something.

The car went back next day!

The Dead Bat Lady
St Joseph, Missouri USA

I lived alone in an apartment in downtown St Joseph, Missouri. The building I lived in was so old that it didn't have any elevators, and I lived on the 10th floor. It was cheap rent, though.

I came home from work really late one night, probably around 11pm. After a full morning of classes, a long shift at work, and climbing all those stairs to get to my apartment, I was ready to just crawl into bed.

The stairs were at the opposite end of the hallway from my apartment and the hall was dimly lit. There were no windows and only a couple of weak bulbs to light the entire hall, so it was always dark no matter what time of day it was.

I blamed the darkness for it being common to encounter bats inside the building, and to occasionally even find one dead in the hall just outside my door. But, like I said, it was cheap rent.

As I turned the corner from the stairs, I saw an old woman standing outside my apartment. She was sort of rocking back and forth, and I thought I could hear her mumbling something. I hadn't lived there more than three months or so, and this was the first time I'd seen or encountered anyone else on the 10th floor. I had the impression that I was the only 10th-floor tenant. Why someone that old would want to live that far up in a building with no elevator was beyond me, but as late as it was I figured she must be a tenant.

As I approached her, I jingled my keys as a hint so she'd move away from my door, but she didn't. She just stood there, rocking back and forth from side-to-side on her feet. And, she was indeed mumbling something.

I cautiously walked up to her and asked her to excuse me, and I reached past her and jiggled the doorknob as a less-subtle hint. The mumbling stopped, and she turned and put her face right in mine. She was a lanky, old woman with a bitter smell to her. I didn't know what to do. Something about her eyes weren't quite right and I quickly looked down at my keys as I fumbled to get my door unlocked. I inserted the key, but suddenly I realized this woman seemed to have the intention of going into my apartment. She turned and faced the door, waiting for me to give the key a final twist.

I stopped, keeping the key in the lock but ready to withdraw it at any second. The tension in the atmosphere was more than I could bear. She hadn't said a word (other than the mumbling), but I could feel an overpowering anger, maybe even actual evil, just emanating from her. Then her body language caught up with the vibes see seemed to be generating. She turned and put her face right in mine again and her eyes got wild. She was either

119

possessed or completely insane. I didn't dare let go of the key, but couldn't withdraw it from the lock without brushing my arm against her -- something I just wasn't willing to do! I was trapped.

I didn't say anything. I just froze. She started to mumble again. It was more than mumbling, though. Being this close to her, I realized she was chanting something. I put my shoulder against the door to create some distance between us and pulled the key from the lock.

I quickly turned to leave, glancing behind me once to see what she was doing. It wasn't a pretty sight. At her feet I could see the body of a dead bat. Right at my door, where I'd found others. Wasn't there a minute ago, it just seemed to drop out of her clothing or something. I don't know where she'd been keeping it, and I don't ever want to know. What I do know is that I wasn't getting a good feeling about any of it.

My eyes had just gotten use to what little light there was by my door, and I was hurrying back into the darkness of the long hall. Ahead of me was another dull light at the stairway. At about three-quarters of the way to the stairs, it suddenly felt as though I had stepped outside of the evil presence that seemed to surround the nasty old woman. I turned again and looked at her. The distance between us gave me a safe feeling, and I called back to her. I told her she needed to leave. Then, for whatever reason, I added, "Jesus is Lord."

At that moment, she took a few steps toward me, and I could make out the angry words, "I'll burn your coffin and dance on your corpse someday." Then she opened the door of the apartment across the hall and shuffled inside. As soon as the door closed, any remaining feelings of tension and evil completely vanished. Passing by the door she entered, I called out a short Bible verse. I don't remember which one. Probably the Lord's Prayer. I continued straight to my apartment and locked myself inside, leaving the bat carcass in the hallway for the maintenance guys to take care of and, after a little praying I fell asleep.

The next morning I called the building manager and told him what had happened, and I told him there was another dead bat outside my door. He said he'd send someone up, and remarked that I must have been asleep for a lot longer than I thought. I asked him what he meant by that, and he told me he knew exactly what crazy old lady I was talking about -- the only other tenant besides me on that floor -- and that he had found her dead in her apartment two days earlier!

I moved out that day.

Perverted Ghost
Hong Kong, Mong Kok China

My uncle told me this story who is a police in Hong Kong.

After working for several years as a police officer he was transfered to a department to crack down on prostitution in Hong Kong.

After several weeks of investigation on an apartment, they were finally convinced that this place was operating illegally and his partner went in as a snitch to hide hidden cameras for evidence.

Police raided the place and arrested two women who were caught in the act but one woman was found naked in a room crying and scared. The woman told them that there was a man who disappeared in the bathroom. They searched the room and bathroom and found no one.

It was after when my uncle was going through the evidence that it shocked him. The video showed the woman entering the room talking to someone. But no one else was seen in the video. In the video the woman was seen taking her clothes off and was performing a sex act in thin air. After she was then seen walking towards the bathroom, she opened the door and screamed.

There were no windows in the bathroom for the man to get away. The only exit was back out to the bedroom.

The story apparently then broke out and it was in many well known magazines in Hong Kong.

The Ghost of a Student
Kathmandu, Nepal

It was the year 1998. My elder brother (Andy) got admission in one of the most prestigious colleges of medical sciences in Southeast Asia.

Volume 1 Ghost Stories from Around the World

He is a hard working student. So my dad was glad that he got admission in the medical school named The Teaching Hospital.

As a medical student in Asia, it's really different from western part of the world. Students work really, really hard there. And my brother was like one of those students. Every night he used to go the study room and study till 4 o'clock in the morning. Whenever he finished his study of the day and try to go to bed, there was always a student who stayed there later than he did. So once Andy talked to this guy and the guy told his name was ANAND SHAH. Shah told Andy that Shah is one of the best students in teaching hospital and he always comes on the top lists of the best students in the college. My brother Andy was impressed. He used to meet Shah everyday and they used to discuss about their book materials. My brother became really good in the studying material.

After a year, my brother became one of the best students of the same college. The college used to take pictures of the students who came under top 10. Then they were invited for a dinner at the principal's place. So as my brother (Andy) went for dinner he saw the picture of Anand Shah. He then smiled and ask principal, "Why isn't Shah invited today??"

Principal replied, "He was one of the best student. But 5 years ago, he couldn't make it as the best student of the year so he committed suicide in the study room. May his soul rest in peace!"

My brother then never went back to the study room

again! But he used to tell me even today nobody can switch off the light in between 3 to 5 am in the morning at the study room. If somebody tries, it would light up again.

Demon Child
Tijeras, New Mexico USA

My story takes place about 12 years ago. I was 15 and spending the summer with my best friend Allan. During the week we would stay at his mother's house which was usually pretty uneventful. But, on the weekends we got to go to his grandma's house.

Allan's Grandma's house was way up in the mountains about an hour from civilization. Her house was the oldest house on the family farm. The farm was completely self sufficient, they grew their own food, raised their own cattle, and everything else that goes along with owning a farm.

Allan's Grandma was about 91 years old and very odd. She would tell us stories about the farm, people dying, ghost sightings, etc. She would really freak us out. She would sit in the living room and talk to an empty chair as if a person was sitting there or lay in bed and whisper to someone and laugh, but no one was ever there.

One night Allan's Grandma told us a story and I'll never forget what happened afterward. She said one day about twenty years ago her son, James, had a horrible experience while riding his horse next to the family cemetery.

James was checking the fence that separated the family property from the neighboring family's property. It was raining outside and the thunder and lightning was starting to get really bad. As James decided to turn around and come home he heard what he described as a young child crying. James slowed his horse to a brisk walk and tried to look through the rain to see if he could see the child. As he came to the cemetery he saw a child sitting in the middle of the field. The child was facing away from him and had a hooded type blanket on, with the hood covering the child's face. James got off his horse and walked over to the child. The child was just rocking back and forth and continually getting louder and louder as it cried. James put his hand on the child's shoulder and asked the child if he could help him. The child immediately stopped rocking back and forth and stopped crying. The child then turned its head completely backwards, while its body stayed facing forward. The child then looked at James. James became horrified, the child was an adult with a gray face and black lips. James couldn't see the eyes but he could see that it was smiling.

James began to run to his horse and fell down in the mud. James got up and made it to his horse. He began to ride away as fast as the horse would run. As James rode away he could hear the child crying as if it was right in his ear. After riding fast and hard for a couple of minutes James had an excruciating pain in both of his sides. James turned around to find the evil crying thing sitting on his horse with him with its hands around his sides. James screamed at it and told it to let him go! As James screamed at it, it cried louder and louder. James turned around once last time to pry the thing off him and saw the hood had fallen down revealing it's head. James said he saw himself in the huge dark red eyes of the thing. James said when the thing noticed James could see its eyes it smiled, and as quickly as it happened it was over. James went home and told his mother what had happened.

After listening to the story Allan and I were pretty scared. We went to our room and talked to each about the story we had just heard. Our room was directly south of the family cemetery and we could see the gates from the moon shining on it. As Allan was talking to me I saw something small moving about in the field. I told Allan and he could see it too. We both stared at it and then it stopped as if it noticed us; I felt terrified. Allan said, "Look it's looking right at us." I could only see what looked like some type of hooded thing walking towards us; then it began to run towards us. Not slowly but really fast, almost abnormally fast - all the while it appeared like it was looking right at us. Allan and I ducked behind the window and right at that moment a loud thump hit the wall outside. Then I heard what sounded like a child crying. I ran as fast as I could to the living room of the house, Allan was right behind me. As I got to the living room and turned the light on I saw that Allan had been so scared he actually pee'd in his pants.

I don't know what we saw and I don't know why we saw it. We told Allan's Grandma the next day and she said it was a demon that had followed her around since she was little and pops up from time to time when she tells that story. The scary part was she said it so matter-of-fact, like if what she had just said was normal.

Allan and I have told this story many times. Some people

believe me, and some don't. I don't care whether people believe it or not. I tell this story because I have never heard a story like it or had an experience like it since. I stopped trying to make sense of it, cause that just freaks me out more.

Haunted Church?
Hants County, Nova Scotia Canada

I have always believed in ghosts. My family, for the most part, has always only believed in the normals in life, what they could see, hear, touch, and explain rationally.

We live fairly close by a very old church and cemetery where I work part time seasonally as a caretaker. It's agreeable work that pays under the table, which is always good.

My father, years ago, told me an interesting story concerning he and his brother when they were much younger. It was late at night, very cloudy, and since it's Nova Scotia, there was a good layer of fog blanketing the land. They were out for a walk, chatting about various chores they had done, when they passed the church. An ominous feeling came over them as they walked by the front walkway of the church. According to my father, they initially just shrugged this off. Everybody has a phobia of graveyards at night for some reason, and they just assumed their imagination was playing tricks on them.

After walking about another mile, they turned around

and started back the way they had came. The way my father described it, as they were nearing the cemetery grounds again, the moon broke free of the cloud cover for a few minutes, and both of them clearly saw a white dog running towards them from the rear fence of the cemetery (the plots get much older, even into the 1830's, the further back you go).

When the clouds shifted again to obscure the moon, the dog couldn't be seen. The way my father put it was that neither one of them were in very good physical condition, yet they ran full out all the way home, which is over a mile, stopping only to catch their breath when their house was in clear sight.

Now I said that I worked part time in the graveyard. I have never minded it, it's a very gorgeous place in the summer time. I just won't be up there at dusk. I learned my lesson the one time that I did.

It was about 7:00 at night, with the sun just setting in the cloudless sky. I had about another hour's worth of work to do, and wanted to get it finished so I didn't have to worry about coming back early the next morning to finish up. I stopped the mower I was using and walked towards the small utility shack behind the church to grab my gas jug.

As I walked, the fragrant smell of freshly cut grass hovering in the air, I couldn't shake the feeling that the church was reproaching me. Something about the blankness of the stained glass windows bothered me to no end. Anybody could have been in there, staring out at me. The doors to the church are not locked, even at night. Now I

Volume 1 Ghost Stories from Around the World

have always been a huge fan of ghost stories, lore, and Stephen King.

I resolutely told myself that I had always had an overactive imagination when it came to this sort of thing. The feeling left me when I went behind the rear wall of the church and I stopped short. The door to the shed was open. Yet I was sure that I had shut and latched it earlier in the afternoon. Granted, a strong gust of wind could blow the latch back. Yet the door swings OUT, not in. Something that the wind could not have done, even if it was gale force.

Without entering the shed at all I poked my arm in and grabbed the gas jug, expecting to find it gone (gas prices are very high here, and full gas jugs are something that any thief would take to empty into his vehicle) As I was walking back across the lawn to where I had left the mower, I felt fine. It was only while I was pouring gas into the small mower, and when I walked the jug back to the shed, that I started to get the feeling that someone was watching me from inside the church. At this point the notion of leaving and coming back the next day seemed very appealing. Especially since from where I was standing the door to the shed seemed to be open again.

A cold wind of fear slowly ran through me. I didn't think of anything supernatural at this point. I thought someone was playing with me, and anyone that would hide in the woods or the church watching me was disturbing to say the very least. Faltering at the wall of the church, I put my hand out and ran it across the smooth painted surface, wanting to feel its solidity and realness. Abruptly I found that I had had enough for one day. Placing the gas jug on the grass, I turned and went back for the mower. I was going to put both in the shed and then get the hell out of here.

Grunting and cursing the weight of it under my breath, I pulled the silent mower towards the church. Once it and the gas jug were safely ensconced in the shed, I shut the door and spun the latch closed. Walking down the side lawn to where my car was parked, that feeling of being observed came back. I turned around and this time gasped out loud. The front door, and inner door of the sanctuary were standing open. Yet If anyone had gone in, I would have heard or seen them.

The last few minutes that I had been actually mowing, my nerves had been strung up so tight that if ANYTHING had moved out of the corner of my eye, I would have registered it. No cars in the parking area. No family wandering the cemetery taking pictures. Just the sound of night birds singing further back in the cemetery.

The crunch of gravel as I walked back up the main path to the front stairs and door of the church... the coolness of the air and the musty smell very old buildings get as I entered the foyer and then the church... all of this I can remember. Nobody was in the church. Nobody was in the small boiler room. Yet as I backed out of the boiler room, I saw in the very corner of my peripheral vision, the rectory door shut softly.

This was when the first real surge of adrenalin slammed through me. Even at this point I had thought it might be a person. Yet now I had doubts. That door is ALWAYS locked unless a church official is using it. Yet as I said I live in a very rural area and there had been no cars in the parking area. As I stood glued to the spot, I heard rustling coming from the room. Did I walk up the aisle and bang on the door? Try the doorknob myself to see if it was unlocked? Perhaps call out? The answer to all of these possibilities was no. I ran.

Slamming both sets of doors shut with backsweeps of my hands, I was in my car and screaming out of there within seconds. If there had somehow been a church official that got dropped off there that day, then I must have scared the life out of him as well. ;)

I do believe that place is haunted. I have taken pictures of the interior, both at night and daylight (no, I wasn't alone at night, what do you take me for? Ha-ha) and both pictures have either defective spots or orbs in them. I have heard, once, and only once, A loud scream come from behind the church at night in the dead of winter. Back in the woods. Nothing like any animal cry I have ever heard. And, the last time a friend of mine and I were in there, he claimed to see something that shook him so bad he ran without me. He was down the path, panting, and yelling for me, by the time I realized he was gone. Some partner, eh? ;)

You can draw your own conclusions from this story. I certainly hope you enjoyed reading it, I tried to make it longer then a paragraph, and yes, I did manage to freak myself out a little in the telling of this story. Perhaps I'll send the pictures in when this app is updated to allow it, or go some night, alone, to take more.....

Joe Kwon's True Ghost Stories

A Ghostly Comrade
Moscow, Oblast Russia

I have experienced this "encounter" approximately six times, in six different locations. It has happened to me on three separate continents. The most recent experience was in Moscow, about three months ago. I do not know how to explain it, or why this should be happening.

Since I was very young, I have been visited from time to time by an entity that I must describe as a "ghost." It is always the same entity, he is always the same in every way.

I do not feel threatened by this entity, in fact, I feel at peace when he appears. He appears solid and substantial, "lifelike" in every way, with the exception that he does not "speak." I do, however, receive a strong "feeling" from him, as though he is trying to communicate with me.

He is man who appears to be in his early to mid thirties. He is about 5'7" in height, with a beard and a mustache.

He is dressed in a black leather jacket that seems to be of a military style cut. It is double breasted, belted, and has epaulets at the shoulder. He wears small, round "pince nez" glasses, and a black visor cap of the same material as the jacket. His pants are black, and are tucked into the tops of knee-high boots. He wears a white shirt and an black tie that seems to be an old-style "cravat".

He wears, always, a single black glove, carrying the other glove in his left hand. His ungloved hand unvaryingly has a lighted cigarette in it. The odor of the tobacco lingers in the room after he is gone.

The most notable and longest period of time he appeared to me was in late 2006, while I was visiting the states. This occurred in Conroe, Texas. I was awakened late at night by the smoke alarm in my apartment. My wife, who was sleeping near me, and our poodle, who was sleeping on the foot of the bed were also awakened.

I made a tour of the house, and finding no fire, checked the battery in the alarm and went back to bed. Ten minutes later, it went off again. I got up, looked around again, and finding nothing, went back to bed.

About an hour later, it went off again. This time, since it was early morning, I did not go back to sleep, but rather lay in bed and just tried to rest. About five or ten minutes later, our little dog began to growl lowly. When I looked up, I saw him standing in the room, watching me. He was standing by the window, in a well lighted area, plainly visible. He nodded toward me, and smiled. My wife, who was asleep beside me, or so I thought, just kept sleeping.

I was immediately overcome with a sense of peace and well-being. I seemed to sense that he was just "checking in" or watching out for me. Shortly, I don't know exactly how much time passed, he departed. He stood erect... he had been leaning against the wall with his arms crossed... turned, and walked out through the window. The window was not open. We were on the third floor. As I watched, he grew smaller and smaller, as if he were receding in the distance.

As soon as he was out of the room, my wife turned to me and asked me, "What happened?" I told her. She said that it was the strangest thing... she had not been asleep, but had been completely unable to open her eyes or to move for about half an hour.

This is only one of the times he has come to me. It began when I was about 14 or 15 years old, living in Center, Texas, and has happened at other times since. He has visited me in Sri Lanka and in Siberia... geography seems to be no concern to him. He has appeared next to me in a car, going down a highway.

On each occasion, I have tried to communicate with him, and gotten a strong feeling... an impression... that he would like to talk to me, but can't, that it's somehow "against the rules." I have also been left, each time he visits, with the strong impression that he is looking out for me and my family in some way.

If you are interested in this experience, I will write down the entire series of events, from the beginning, as well as I remember them, and post them later.

Just before he departs, he always smiles at me, and "salutes" by touching the visor of his cap with the glove he carries in his hand.

The House On Attawandaron Road
London, Ontario Canada

I moved in when I was thirteen and stayed until I was sixteen (I am now eighteen). All my life I've been sensitive to paranormal activity, but in all my life I have never encountered such chaos as at this house.

So many occurrences, I would be unable to type them all, but here are a few:

In some photos of me, behind me is what appears to be a mask. I have (on three occasions) had poltergeist actions(Kleenex box cover thrown at me and just missed my head, a pot knocked of the shelf in the dead of the night and slammed onto the floor near the hallway, big glass sliding back door thrown open, after I locked it). We have heard moans, groans and large gasps for air (not a lingering spirit reliving an occurrence, it was there to scare and bother us, this I knew). Knocks on windows, a white light on the floor even zooms by out of the corner of my eye.

Lights turn on and off. And on two occasions, walking by the ravine by the house, we were chased by that invisible entity. I was scared by the form of a huge black mean dog hunched over under the stairs, snarling and threatening me (that was in the basement).

The most horrifying of all was when I was awakened by a dark shadow next to and above my bed, touching my private parts in a manner of something I have never felt.

This house was not a pleasant place. Even my two cats were tormented on a regular basis. Lindsay my room-mate was targeted by them. They would try to scare her by sending her feelings of death and turning around and slowly walking into my room up the hall. They did this so that she would think that I was in danger. We were not naive to energy and spirits and did everything in our power to remove the problem. The energy seemed to be in the core/center of the house, which were the stairwells to basement, first and second floor. It went everywhere, but was the strongest there and in the (ugh!) basement.

We were so tortured by this that night after night, we'd sit in dark corners together shaking with terror and hold knives to protect ourselves. And at times we slept in the same bed, it was better than suffering alone. Nightmares and night-terrors also seemed to find us. I don't know if it's significant, but the house was on Indian territory and ten doors down from the Indian museum and old camp site.

It was a semi-detached home, with some major hauntings. After leaving I discovered that most (if not all) of my power of sensing and reading energy and my ability to communicate with my spirit guides had vanished, so I 've done what I can to regain it and we have promised ourselves never to return to that house on Attawandaron road, or the Indian area.

Footprints
Toronto, Ontario Canada

I will start by saying that the location I used is my current city of residence, not the city I saw the ghosts in. I have also changed the names of the people involved.

Before immigrating to Canada, I lived in the Middle East. My parents would take me and my older brother to the park every weekend. They'd meet up with their friends who had three daughters. Us five kids (the three sisters, my brother, and I) would play while our parents smoked and gossiped.

There seems to be less concern about safety regulations in that country and they are less strictly followed than in North America. Behind the park, there was a school, with only a chain link fence separating the two. The school was deserted after a fire that had occurred there many years ago.

The idea of entering a deserted school terrifies me now at the age of sixteen but at that time I was only ten years old, and I find that kids are a lot braver than most adults. My brother Jon, the three sisters Lily, Mary, and Alice and I would always crawl through a hole in the fence, scamper through the school grounds, and enter the school through the only door not boarded up, excited for a day of playing teacher and exploring the abandoned school ruins.

Our parents did not know that we went inside the school until one day when Jon tripped and a shard of glass from a broken window cut though his palm. He was rushed to the hospital and we were forbidden from going into the school again. Our parents didn't like the idea of five kids playing in deserted classrooms, breaking rusted locks off lockers, and picking pieces of chalk off the dusty, glass-ridden hallways.

We stayed away for a while, but the temptation of the school, which we regarded as our own private playhouse, was too great for us to resist. We kept frequenting the school until one summer day...

As far as we knew, no one else went in the school, so we were very surprised to see two boys during one of our adventures. I remember to this day, six years later, exactly what they looked like. One was taller than me and the other was a whole head shorter. They both wore dirty, torn clothes. One was barefoot. The other was wearing a scorched pair of sneakers. On one foot, his toes poked through.

Lily, who was twelve at the time, was the first to speak up. As the eldest child there, we saw her as a leader of sorts. "Where did you come from?" she asked them.

The shorter boy was the one to reply. "Upstairs."

This sparked a lot of curiosity in us. None of us had ever been on the second floor of the school. All the stairs had burned down in the fire. We told them that it was impossible since there were no stairs. We had come in through the school's only entrance.

"It doesn't matter," the taller boy said. "You have to

leave."

This made us very defensive and I snapped at the guy, "Listen, this is OUR school. I'm not gonna let a street kid tell me what to do. You don't even have proper shoes on," I said, looking down at his ripped shoe as I mocked him.

The two boys began walking towards us. I vaguely heard one of them say, "You will leave, now, or bad things will happen." I was too horrified at what I was seeing... although they were walking on a floor littered with dust and broken glass they were leaving no footprints. Shock was setting in when I screamed "GUYS, LET'S GO!" and ran out of the school at full speed. They followed me out asking what was wrong, but I was crying too hard to say anything. I ran to my parents. They calmed me down and I told them what happened.

Predictably, my dad said I was being silly. The next week, my dad took me back to the school to show me that there was nothing to fear. When we got there, we were surprised to see construction workers all around the school. Upon inquiry, one of them told us, "Last Friday, the hallway ceiling collapsed. We're demolishing the whole school." I started crying again because that was the day the two ghosts told us to leave. If it weren't for them, the five of us would be buried under the collapsed ceiling, most likely dead.

It's a rare day that goes by when I don't think of the apparitions that saved my life on that summer day in the Middle East. I am so grateful. Thank you.

Joe Kwon's True Ghost Stories

The Cemetery Demon
Toronto, Ontario Canada

I don't know if this is a ghost story or not. I don't know what it is. But it happened to my brother and I about two years ago.

We were in a cemetery because it was nearby and that was the cool thing to do. I started to feel spooked, so I asked my brother if we could leave, and we were leaving when at that same moment we saw something in the sky.

It was initially hidden by trees, but we heard something flapping and swooshing and couldn't really tell anything about it. Except that it seemed larger than a bird.

And then we saw it. We clearly saw it was a man in black strange clothes, twisting awkwardly like he didn't do that very often. He couldn't fly well. It was apparent he was trying to get somewhere, but wasn't getting where he wanted.

Well we ran. Of course. I was terrified and nothing seemed to work but my legs. I couldn't scream, though I would have if I could. My brother was only two steps in front of me.

We were through the gate and well away from the cemetery before we stopped from sheer exhaustion. Only then did we look back. The road we were on was up higher than the cemetery, one reason that we had to stop, because we were running up hill. Looking back down, we could see the man or creature or whatever again. He swooped a few times.

Suddenly he went all the way down to the the ground. I couldn't see him anymore. But it was only seconds. Seconds, and he came back up into view.

And when he came up we saw that he was carrying a body. More silhouette than anything, but I could tell he was carrying a man, holding him with his hands in the man's armpits. And the man was limp, not moving. I thought it obvious, that it went without saying, that he had a dead man from the cemetery. I just somehow knew it.

Me and my brother were so shocked we couldn't move. The man carrying the man flew away into the darkness and the distance. At some point we just started running again. We didn't even have to say Go. We both starting running at the same instant and didn't stop until we were home.

My brother and I haven't talked about it. Not even to each other. We met each other's eyes a few times and knew what the other was thinking. But it was too frightening. We can't talk about it. I need to let it go, pretend it didn't happen. When I got this app, I thought maybe telling about it would help me get past it.

In Good Hands
Enschede, Overijssel Netherlands

On the 9th of October, 2007, my grandmother died. It was

a rainy day, and there was a very strange atmosphere around our town. I was so sad that I'd lost her.

Then October the 9th came again... it was now 2008. I didn't even notice it was the day my grandmother died, but I noticed this strange atmosphere around our town again that was there the day she passed away.

I didn't pay attention to it very much, and I walked up the stairs to get something from my bedroom. When I opened the door, there she was. My grandmother. She was sitting on my bed, and looked peaceful and pleased.

It scared the crap out of me, and I ran downstairs again. I told my boyfriend about it, and he walked with me upstairs again. When we opened the door again, she was gone. I told my boyfriend where I saw her and walked towards my bed.

When I looked at my bed, I saw the spot where she was sitting. You could see somebody had sat there, and the spot was all warmed.

I have never seen her since then, but the sight of her peaceful face made me realize she is in good hands, and she is okay... but still, it was a very strange experience.

The Closet Mirror
Oxford, Oxfordshire England

In 2008 I was in a deep sleep when I awoke with my 8 year-old son Ben poking my arm repeating, "Daddy." It was

12:30, so I moaned, "What's wrong, Sport?" He grabbed my arm as tightly as he could and whispered in my ear, "It's in the closet!"

I got out of bed and noticed that Ben was so scared he could pee in his pants! I assumed it was just a nightmare that little kids get. I soon found out how wrong I was.

I walked up to his room and tucked him in, and left the light on so he could easily see me go into the closet and prove that nothing was there. I opened the door and I was right, for now! Nothing was in the closet. But when I was closing the door Ben screamed, and it wasn't any old scream, it was a scream that a parent could never forget!

I twirled around and asked him what was wrong. He said nothing, only pointed at the mirror. I turned around to see a figure, human shape, but you could tell it wasn't human. The figure held something in its hand and its eyes stared at Ben and it pointed at him.

In a panic to protect my son, I grabbed Ben's desk chair and broke the mirror. My wife awoke to the horrible sound, running upstairs only to find a broken mirror, Ben crying into my chest gripping onto my back/shirt, and me holding him. I looked up at my wife whose face said it all: what the hell is going on here and is Ben okay?

I told her to go back to bed and I would tell her in the morning. She agreed and walked down stairs, "Ben, you should sleep with me tonight," I said. He looked up and nodded, and just seeing the terror in his face made me want to cry.

1 year later.

People came to our house and informed us that their grandparents lived here, and they used to visit here as a child. She asked if she could come in, and my wife and I agreed to let her inside. When she walked by Ben's room, she said, "Oh... I remember this room." I saw her face and asked, "Is that a bad thing?" She asked if we could talk alone. I agreed and so we went to my study.

She told me that her dad had a horrible medical condition (I don't remember what the illness is called but she informed me that your brain didn't function properly and would replace your bones with bones that were misshaped bones and your body would be deformed.)

She said that while he was alive he would look in the closet mirror and tell her over and over again, "I want to be young, I never had a normal childhood with perfect bones, want to be a perfect boy."

I then realized that the thing in the mirror a year ago was her dad. He was deformed and he wanted my son, because he has a perfect bone structure and he can have a normal childhood. When I broke the mirror he was gone because he only said that to the closet mirror.

Working In The Plantation
Pago Pago, American Samoa

This story is a recollection based on a true story of what

happened to one of my aunts.

It was 1981 and my aunt, who was 10 at the time, was working in the family's taro plantation. It was 7 p.m. and gradually getting dark. It was quite superstitious for a young girl to be working the plantation, though my aunt didn't care much for superstition. She kept working for a further half an hour, until she became tired. However, she had not finished the work that she was asked to do.

As my aunt was catching her breath, she was suddenly greeted by an old man. The old man was dressed in a traditional Samoan cloth (ie lavalava) and he looked like he had just finished a day of work in another plantation. My aunt was stunned at first, she was puzzled as to where the man had come from. The surrounding neighborhood was very small, so everyone had known each other. My aunt did not recognize him.

He started some small talk. He asked my aunt about which family line she comes from, what her name was, and why she was out in the plantation alone. She told him that she had to finish off cleaning and uprooting the taro crops as part of her share of chores.

He asked if she needed some help with her work. My aunt agreed as she was tired. They both worked on the plantation until gradually the work was all done. My aunt was glad and grateful to the old man for his help, and thanked him. The old man did not budge, he had no smile nor did the tone in his voice change, it was pretty much the same monotone voice. After my aunt thanked him, he paused and looked right into her face and told her to never tell anyone in the village that she had seen him, nor that he helped her with the work. In addition, he told her that the minute she tells anyone, she would go insane. My aunt did not know what to say, she said thanks once again, and started to walk home from the plantation. The old man walked off into the night while whistling. He disappeared.

My aunt arrived home and told her mum (my grandma) what had happened, and about the old man. My grandmother told my aunt a story of an old man who used to work in the plantation 15 years before. He had a heart attack and died while uprooting crops. The only person to see him die was his grand daughter, who was 8 at the time. She was helping him with the plantation, and she never spoke to anyone about what happened.

The next night my aunt started to hear distant cries and wailing. It was a little past midnight. She woke up and went to get a glass of water, and as she did that she walked into the bathroom. Since there was no light in the bathroom, she used a candle. As she walked into the bathroom, she suddenly stopped in shock. In the mirror, standing behind her and staring right at her with wide eyes, was the old man clutching his heart.

Singing Lady
Paris, France

It all started about 2:00 AM in the morning. I share a room with my little brother. My whole family had gone to bed and I had just finished watching a movie on t.v and decided to go to bed.

I made my way up to my bedroom, put on my bed clothes, and hopped into bed. It was not until about ten minutes after that I heard a voice that sounded to be singing. I could not make out who or what was making the noise, but it seemed to be coming from the attic. I went up the stairs and made my way into the attic, thinking I had left a radio on or some such.

As I got to the top, I saw something I will never forget. There was a lady sitting in the corner in my rocking chair wearing a large gray cape. She looked sort of misty. I was so scared that I ran down the stairs and into my mum and dad's room. They asked me what the matter was, but I did not tell them. In fact, I have not told any one up until this day.

Disturbing a Spirit in Thailand
Pataya, Thailand

This story happened to me 2 years ago when I was 22. At the time I was in a hotel in Thailand.

Before I went I was in Hong Kong, and many of my friends warned me to respect people and be careful when purchasing goods because it was a country known for cursing people. Plus I was told many stories about hauntings in Thailand. I believe in ghosts but never saw one so didn't think much of the stories

Being young and out in Thailand with friends we got drunk a couple of times and may have caused some disturbances.

Anyway it started when one night when we returned to the hotel. We got to the lift where many people were waiting. We were last to step in to the lift and when I stepped in it was overweight and started beeping. I offered to step out and told them I would meet them in the room.

I waited for the next one and stepped in myself. I stayed on the 10th floor. On the 4th floor the lift stopped and the doors opened. No one was there and the whole corridor was dark. On the left there was a set of glass doors where I saw an indoor swimming pool. I didn't think much of it and pressed the button for the lift doors to close.

That night when we were sleeping I heard rattling that woke me. When I looked up I faintly saw a woman standing outside the bathroom. I thought it was one of my friends who stayed in the room next to ours so I asked what she was doing in here so late. But the woman didn't answer and faded away. Freaked out I just covered my head with the covers and started praying until I fell asleep, when I felt more at ease.

The next morning I woke up and a lot of hair was on my pillow. I was worried and told them what I saw last night but they reassured me that I was just dreaming and the hair problem was common.

I also told them that I saw a swimming pool in the 4th floor and we should try it out, but when we got to the 4th floor it was just a corridor with more rooms. After enquiring with the receptionist she told us they only had an outdoor swimming pool. My friends said I was going crazy and we laughed it off.

But after that night I would wake up every morning to have more and more hair coming off on my pillow. I was beginning to have bald patches everywhere. I decided to see a doctor when I returned back to the UK.

In Hong Kong my mum had no idea what was going on with my hair and all. But when she went to a temple to pray, she was speaking to a fortune teller and he told her that someone in her family has attracted or disturbed a female spirit who has been ripping his or her hair out. He also went into details saying she drowned in a hotel swimming pool.

When my mum found out about my hair she freaked out and told me the whole story. After that my Mum went back to the fortune teller asking for help. He said he needed to find out how I disturbed this spirit or how she has chosen me to pick on. She told him I was in Thailand, then out of no where he asked her if I have urinated in a street corner or knocked over any incense bowls. I did urinate in a street corner when I was drunk one night in Thailand.

He then told her apparently many spirits hide or stand about in dark street corners and many Chinese people know to say please excuse me if they were going to urinate in a street corner. I was then given a jade buddha to wear. After wearing it my hair started growing back.

149

So please respect the afterlife and don't do anything foolish when on a drunken night out. You never know what you might disturb.

Marked By a Dream
Bayamon, Puerto Rico

This is a true story believe it or not.

It happened about 24 years ago to my dad. He was a 12 years old child. One night he was asleep and had a dream about being a war prisoner. In the dream he was marked by a hot iron with letters to identify him as a prisoner.

He woke up with a sharp pain on his leg. The mark of the letters was there; red and angry.

24 years later, he still has the fading scar on his leg.

I honestly can't explain it, and neither can he. We think it may be connected to my grandma (his mom) reading the Ouija Board thus attracting spirits.

The Lonely House
Gurabo, Puerto Rico

First of all, I have to say that I love ghost stories since I was a child. But especially true ghost stories, that is why I am sharing with you my experience.

I live in Puerto Rico, it is a beautiful island in the Caribbean. It is full of legends of mystery about our history. Interesting stories about haunted places, cemeteries, abandoned houses, legends of pirates and so on.

My dad loved to gather with me and my brother at night to tell spooky stories. We always started laughing, but in the end it was kind of scary.

Especially about a solitary house which was surrounded by only vegetation near his childhood home. He had to go by the house every time he left his home. He started telling us about the strange sightings that appeared in the windows, but most of the time in the upper one.

He told us about one kid that went inside alone while his friends waited outside. Time passed, they got worried and they all went inside looking for him. They say he was in the second floor staring blankly at the window. They called him, he jumped and screamed all the way outside the house.

They asked him about what he saw. He was shaking and he said that when he opened the door he saw this old man walking up the stairs. He called him because he kind of looked fragile and thought about offering help. But when he reached him, the man turned around, looked at him and asked him to follow him. He does not understand why and how he followed him because he looked kind of weird.

He followed the old man to the room and when they got there the man stared at the window for a couple of minutes. He turned around, looked at him again and went to the window and just disappeared. The kid just stood there in shock. Could not move, talk, scream, nothing came out of him.

I asked my dad a couple of questions, but mostly wanted him to take us to the house. He just laughed and changed the subject.

But of course I'm not a child anymore and went with my boyfriend to check it out. The drive was about 2 hours long. We joked about everything, how stupid we are, believing the silly stuff my dad told us about. We were just having fun until we reached the house.

This is a house built approximately 60 to 70 years ago, and like my dad said it is a lonely haunted spooky house in the middle of nowhere...

Highway Spirit
Lahore, Punjab Pakistan

This happened a year ago when our neighbors where coming back home from another city. They were driving on a long road at night, the road was deserted usually and was surrounded by many trees and was the only route to reach home. It was very late around 2 a.m. in morning. They saw a woman standing in the middle of the road. She was wearing white and had a abnormally long face and hands.

My uncle instantly knew she was not human as he had heard incidents from people who had seen something similar to this woman, and she made no effort to move out the way of the car and just kept staring at them. He drove over her and when he looked from the rear view mirror she was still standing there, in the same place looking after the car.

Jinn Encounter in the Woods
Lahore, Punjab Pakistan

Some background information about me: I have always been attracted to the feeling of fear, to an extent. I'm not the type that goes around poking, I don't think I will ever be brave enough for that. However, I do believe in ghosts or Jinn, and spirits, and I respect their space and let them be.

So anyway, the story starts out on a dark night when I was about 12 years old. My grandfather and grandmother visited us on numerous accounts. I used to tell them stories to keep them busy and not bored. But I was really bored one night... bored of watching T.V and of everything else. My grandfather absolutely LOVED to tell stories to everyone about his life. So that night I decided to ask him to tell me a scary story for a change. I thought he would tell me one of the stories he read from a newspaper that he really liked as was his custom, but he promised to tell me a personal account of a ghost story if I promised I wouldn't get too scared. I agreed. So here is his story:

It takes place way back in the day when he was just starting out his family with my grandmother. It takes place in Pakistan when it first partitioned from India and it was not so densely populated as it is now. New neighborhoods were forming and people were moving from India to Pakistan and vice-versa with whatever they could carry on their backs. It so happened that my grandfather heard of a new neighborhood that was forming in Lahore, Pakistan. He decided that it would be a good start to move his family and begin a new and fresh life. Now remember, Lahore is to Pakistan as New York is to the United States nowadays but back then, it was newly developing so the new neighborhood that my grandfather found the house in had about 2-3 houses in it. All the houses were surrounded by thick woods. Since it just developed, there were no streets, or streetlights, and thus no personal transportation could have been used. But it had a bright and promising future.

Well time went on and everyone in the tiny neighborhood got to be familiar with each other and my grandpa and one of the neighbors found jobs as heads of a train conductor company. He had to get up at 4am and leave to work when it was still dark out. Well, he told me that sometimes he used to catch up with his neighbor and walk to work jointly through the woods in the morning. Since it was still early morning and dark outside, both of them provided each other company. They used to have to carry lanterns to pierce the darkness enveloping the woods. By the time they got out of the woods, morning light would start shining through.

Well on this particular night, my grandfather started walking to work carrying his lantern as usual. In the distance in front of him he saw a bright light like that of a lantern and figured that it was his neighbors lantern, so he decided to catch up to him and walk together as they always did. Because it was very dark due to the thick woods and the distance, he could only see the light from the lantern and not the figure holding it. He started running to catch up to him and called out his name. However, he said that his neighbor didn't stop to wait for him. Rather, the faster he ran to catch up with him, the faster the light progressed and kept the same distance between them. So my grandfather assumed that his neighbor didn't hear him and called his name out several more times.

He kept running after him but the same thing kept happening: the more he would run to catch up with him, the more it looked like the lantern light the neighbor was carrying ran forward. When my grandfather ran one more time to catch up with him, he finally saw his neighbor stop to wait for him. Only, when he got a little closer, he saw that it wasn't his neighbor. He said he saw the light/fire stop, but when he got close enough, but still maintaining a distance, he saw that there was no one holding the light there was only the odd light hovering in mid air. The light then turned into a big figure, which he described looked like a lion or bear but had two glowing eyes. It looked like the glowing eyes were fixed on him. He realized that he thought one of the eyes was his neighbor's lantern. Boy, how wrong he was.

At this point he started getting scared because he knew that he had disturbed something that he shouldn't have. He said that he felt scared for his life and felt like the figure was angry with him. What scared him worse was that the figure with the glowing eyes started moving toward him. He thought about running but instinct told him that it would be no good. It was as if he was dazed and couldn't move. As it got closer, he started freaking out. He then remembered some verses of the Quran that could be read in times of danger to ward off evil spirits or the like. He started saying the verses out loud. As soon as he started praying, the figure stopped, turned around, and proceeded like it had before, going the way it had originally been heading before my grandpa had stopped it. He told me that he waited there for a while until he thought it was safe to proceed. He then managed to walk the rest of the way to work but was very cautious walking through the rest of the woods through the crack of dawn.

He finished his day of work but what had happened earlier was still on his mind. He wanted to find out what had happened so he contacted a religious Mullah/priest and asked him to shed some light on what happened earlier. The Mullah told him that when he was walking through the woods, a procession of Jinns were passing through to attend morning prayer called Fajar Namaz

(Muslims pray 5 times a day and the morning prayer is called Fajar Prayer, which is performed when the sun rises). He said that they wanted to be left alone but when he kept running after them they got angry and wanted to harm him. They were about to, but when my grandfather said the prayer, they heard it and backed off and went their own way again. The Mullah told him that if it were not for the prayer, he would have been harmed that day.

After that day, my grandfather always made sure that his neighbor would meet at him at his house before work and then walk together. Later on, the neighborhood formed streets and lights and much more houses were built in the midst of the bustling city it is today, so there were many other methods and options to get to work rather than walking through the woods at night. Now it is a major city of Pakistan. However, there still are a good amount of stories about Jinn and spirits as well as black magic that still take place.

If you want to know more about Jinn, you could look it up on the web. Muslims believe that Jinn are just like people in the matter of choices. The closest thing they resemble in the English language would be something like ghosts. They are also free to choose their religion and beliefs and will be judged on judgment day just like human beings. There are good and bad in them as well. They have societies and there are many different types of them. They live among us but we cannot see them, however they could see us. They are made from a smoke-less fire.

According to the Quran, God placed a veil/curtain behind our eyes so we cannot see them. My friend recently told me that there is a Surah (chapter) in the Quran that if it is read three times, the veil/curtain will be lifted. My personal belief tells me that it would be terrifying. I don't know why people would personally attempt to do such a thing. Ive heard that once the veil behind your eyes has been lifted, and you become afraid of the Jinn you see, then they control you, but if you are not afraid of them, then you could control them. I wouldn't advise this to anyone and that's why I haven't included which Surah to read, so please dont ask me which Surah it is. I know black magic is widely known in countries like Pakistan. There are people that are known to control Jinns. Well this is getting long so I will stop although I have much more to tell.

There's no doubt this story is true, my grandfather doesn't make up stories, he is a very factual man. Decide for yourself. My mom also told me about her mother (my grandmother), and how someone cursed her when my mom was young. It was a terrifying experience for all of her siblings as well as herself. Ill leave that story for another day. I hope you guys enjoyed this. Feel free to leave me comments and let me know if you want me to write about what happened with my grandmother. Any comments/suggestions would be appreciated! I reply back ASAP. Thanks for reading!

Poltergeist
Lahore, Punjab Pakistan

I heard this story from my grandmother and I have not experienced any of it..

Volume 1 Ghost Stories from Around the World

For 15 years ago I visited my grandmother in Pakistan after my grandfather passed away. The story goes back to early 1930 when there was no Pakistan and all was India under British rule. My family was landlords, still are and we had the largest lands in India.

I was told that my grandfather was out for hunting in his land with some British generals. That area was a thick jungle and tigers were the main target. I was told that according my grandfather the jungle was very calm. Hardly any sound or noise.

During dawn, my grandfather and the generals were heading back to the camp by foot. In front of them the porters were leading the way until they suddenly halted and stopped singing.

In front of them (I do not know the distance), there was a very beautiful woman standing with a white sari. There was a sudden standstill and everyone was scared. What was this woman doing in the middle of the forest.

My grandfather asked her from a distance if all was ok. He was slowly approaching her and stopped when he saw her eyes. According to him, that was the blackest eyes he ever seen, if she had any eyes? He also noticed that her feet were twisted so basically the toes was on the back. That of course scared him and he asked once again who she was, but this time raising his gun. The answer was the highest scream kind of laugh he ever heard and suddenly the woman attacked the hunting crowd while giving a high pitched scream.

And as she attacked she vanished.

Once all reached the camp, most of the people developed fever including my grandfather.

When my grandfather finally was home his fever was getting better but somehow he took the part of the jungle home.

My grandmother told me that all started with someone knocking on the front door very loud. When the guard opened the door, no one was there. It kept going for days and our guards was losing patience.

My grandmother thought that someone was playing a prank. They did wonder how the doorknocker hid so fast. The house was more like a palace with massive gardens and guards everywhere. How could that person sneak in and do all the pranks.

But one day all the prank ideas went out of the roof. During the evening time one of the kitchen workers screamed. My grandmother went to the kitchen to see what was going on. She said that all the kitchen units and chairs were stacked up and all the knives balancing on their tips.

Couple of days went on and all seemed to be back to normal. And then of course the knocking started again. This time the guards had an idea how to catch the knocker. They spread flour all over the garden, next to the main door and if someone knocked on the door, they will see on what direction the person is coming from and where he is hiding. That same night they heard the bangs on the front door and the guard opened the door to see in what direction the knocker went. The biggest surprise was that they only saw three footsteps leaving the door and nothing else. That of course freaked them out.

My grandmother said the knocking and the kitchen activities were occurring on a regular basis and after a while stones started hailing the house.

They all were getting tired and they requested a priest into their house. I was told that once the priest started the prayers they heard screams and doors shutting and opening. All stopped when the ballroom mirror crashed.

After that, nothing more was experienced.

What I found interesting was that I do not believe in ghosts, but I have seen a lot of movies with similar events. I know for sure that my grandmother has not. Sadly she passed away the day after my wedding and she was a highly respected woman. What she or my grandfather experienced happened over 70 years ago.

I do not believe in poltergeists but it sounds like one.

Santa Maria Del Mexicano (Boarding School)
Colon, Queretaro Mexico

Well I'm 17 years old now, but this happened to me a year ago at this boarding school. It was a night like any other night and just like all nights bedtime was at 9:30p.m. It was around 20-30 people and I in one dorm room with one person in charge of putting everyone to bed and keeping us silent.

On this night I was with two other kids in the dorm and we kept talking and laughing so much that the one in charge got mad at us and sent the 3 of us to sleep in the shower room with a lock so we couldn't get out at night.

So there we were in this wet and dirty looking shower room with nothing to do. The three of us finally decided to fall asleep. I remember the order of how we slept... one kid slept on one side of the room, one kid in the middle, and me on the other side of the room. I think we all fell asleep easily, but after awhile I started to wake up because I felt a breeze or a hand sliding on my upper left thigh. I quickly woke with a fright because I thought it was a large rat or some type of large insect crawling on my leg. I was scared but I didn't turn on the light that was just above me because I figured whatever it was it had gone away and I was really tired anyways.

I looked at what time it was on my watch before I went back to bed and the time read 4:00a.m. So I started sleeping again, but after just 5 to 10 minutes I felt that same breeze, that same crawling on my face. I woke wide awake with my eyes staring straight up. This time I knew it was a hand. I quickly got up this time more afraid than the first and started to move my blanket, my pillow, and everything around me like crazy.

I quickly stood up turned on the lights which woke my

friends up. Neither of them was close enough to have touched me. They just looked at me like I was crazy and they told me to just go back to bed. I agreed and turned off the lights, but I really didn't want to go to sleep anymore because I feared whatever was in this shower room would just come and wake me up again.

But I started fading into sleep again then it morning and everything was just normal again but now at nights I always go to sleep without making a sound so the one in charge won't make me fall asleep in the shower room. He told me if I start acting bad again at sleeping hours next time he'll make me sleep in the shower room alone.

The Black Shadow
Rhodes, Greece

It all started the summer of 1997 and still continues.

My mother and I were coming home from work. It must have been about 12:00pm. Suddenly Mom stopped and looked towards some rosebushes outside our front door.

"I saw you," were her words. I looked at her and asked her what was she talking about. She told me that she saw a shadowy bald man with a hunchback run into the bushes. I didn't think much on it the first time.

A lot of people that visit my house have seen the shadow. It will appear in front of my friends' motorbikes and scare them to the point that they lose control of the bike, and other times they have seen it run past the outside of the house.

I never saw it inside the house, until one day when I was alone in the living room watching television. It must have been 9:00pm, and I was waiting for a friend to come pick me up.

Suddenly I saw a shadow run from one side of the living room to the other side and up the stairs where our bedrooms are. I froze and just watched it run by.

It was exactly how Mom said it was, only I saw it a little clearer. I noticed the sharp nails and hunched back, along with the bald head and pointy ears.

I swear this is true and it scared the hell out of me. Now, from time to time I get strange feelings that what we have in our house is watching me and it's dangerous. Just a few weeks ago it scared my mom almost to death when it ran by her, almost pushing her over, and went down the stairs to the living room.

I don't know what to do about all this but I hope I find an end to it.

The Demon Head
Bidadari Road, Singapore

This is a strange story of my friend Lily.

When Lily was in her teens, she liked to spent her free time at her grandma's room for reading books, because she told me that the room had some kind of deathly silence once you go in. But, her granny did not wish to allow any one in when she was around.

This is what Lily told about an unexpected experience for her. One day, Lily was back home after school as normal. When she entered her house and called her mother, that is what usually Lily does, there was no reply. So she thought her mum might have gone down to shop.

Lily lived in a village, in a wooden house surrounded by banana trees and bushes. While she prepared for a shower she heard a knocking noise from her grandma's room and it sounded something like a bouncing ball in the room. Lily got confused, because there were no kids in her family. Then who was that? Lily wondered. She went down to look. There the strange things happened.

The door opened itself before she reached the door knob. Suddenly she backed off when she could feel cool and icy feelings like some one blew on her face. Then, somehow Lily got brave enough to go in. Once she entered, what a strange thing she saw. A rotten head with long hair flew all over the room and hit on the walls as it went. The eye she saw was very red; there was no eye ball or nose.

My friend was frightened once she saw the bodiless head flying around. After that she collapsed. When she was conscious, she was on the bed beside her family members. Lily didn't tell any one about the strange thing, but she stopped entering Granny's room from that day on.

But, later she came to know by her mother that her granny was a witch for a long time and used the demon head and gave it her own blood drops, for in response it provided whatever granny requested.

But granny suffered before she died and her death was not like an ordinary person's.

The Locket
Marsiling, Singapore

Recently I ran away from home and rented a room nearby. It was quite old and downstairs is a basketball court. After I moved in I had this weird dream over and over again every single night about a couple who were madly in love with each other. The girl was young and in high school. The boy was graduated and owns a bike. Every day after school he would pick up the girl.

There was this period that he was being late real often. The girl started to get angry. She pestered and asked him what happened and always got the same answer that he overslept. They had become distanced over the months.

There came a time when the girl had to go to a certain place and asked the boy to fetch her. This time the boy took 3 hours. She was so angry waiting in a shelter with heavy rain that she demanded a clear explanation from him. He paused for a long while and gave the same answer: I slept overtime.

Volume 1 Ghost Stories from Around the World

The girl was about to hurl remarks at him when the guy whipped out a heart locket necklace and gave her. She saw the grim expression on the guy, and not questioning him further, she accepted the necklace sadly and let him send her home.

They were both quiet, I could still remember tears were trickling down the face as the girl knows this will be the last time they ever meet and it was all over.

Certain time passed and one day she got a call from the boy's mum saying that he had passed on. She was shocked and depressed, living on regretfully, yet to this day she still didn't understand why.

At this point I always wake up with tears flowing down my cheeks. It made me feel wanting to cherish the person I love so I went home and did not have the dream after.

Just on a fateful night I was walking along the basketball court with my boyfriend and saw this girl standing near the court looking up the flats with tears tickling down. Behind her was a boy talking to her softly, but she couldn't seem to hear. I told my boyfriend that we should walk on the other side and leave the couple alone. But my boyfriend was confused and asked me, "What couple? I only see a girl."

I was both frightened and confused myself.

The boy was shouting repeatedly but the girl couldn't hear. Not able to control myself, I shouted, "He said don't cry and open the locket!" She turned around shocked. Goosebumps rose when I realized she was the girl from my dreams. The pale guy turned to me and said thank you. Smiled, and was gone.

She opened the locket and there was a letter that read: I did not mean to be late. I had a heart attack... I'm sorry but I loved you dearly and never forget you. If one day you see this letter, you will know that I will always be with you, in your heart. Don't cry for me as I went to a better place.

The Clone
Singapore

I am a regular soldier that has served the army for the past ten years. During my services, I have encountered several supernatural events that changed my perception of them (ghosts). What I am going to share with you guys now, is one of my encounters.

This whole event occurred in a training ground located in Singapore. I still remember that the time was 2 a.m. in the morning, whereby the troops are resting to prepare for their training in the later part of the day.

I was walking around the training ground to ensure that everyone was sleeping. It was during this time that I heard a faint voice whispering. Wondering why, at this wee hour, that there was still someone not sleeping, I walked towards the direction of the whisper. As I approached the location, the air literally got colder and colder, and the faint outline of a soldier kneeling in front of a big tree, whispering, got clearer and clearer.

I got angry and shouted at him: "Hey dude, it is 2 a.m. and why ain't you resting?" However, there was no response. I got curious and went closer, and this time round I got a clear view of him. Suddenly, he turned back and to my horror, that was me that was kneeling in front of the big tree. I picked up my knee and ran towards the HQ, waking up my friends in the process. However, I did not tell them about my encounter. I just directly went to sleep, not wanting to think further.

In the later part of the day, I went to the same location again. In front of that tree there are several offerings, and from the location of the tree a big cemetery can be seen. However, it doesn't explain my sighting the previous night.

Till today, the image still lingers around in my mind.

Ready or Not Here I Come
Woodlands, Singapore Singapore

Recently I'm having dreams of my past. I had not thought about this incident for a long time. Lately some incidents caused my buried memories to rise again.

It was then I followed a good friend of mine and took care of some volunteer works for the orphanage. Being around children makes me relaxed and happy always. It was play time and we decided to play catch. I was "it".

We had fun and just when we were ready to start a new game this little girl came up telling me that I forgot to

169

"catch" her. I was confused but maybe I had counted wrong. So we started the game and everyone hid. I counted to 10 and turned. I almost got scared when this little girl was standing right behind me. Without thinking, I pointed at her and said, "It". I turn around and ran.

"Ready or not here I come..." Followed by a trail of giggles. It sent chills down my spine.

Suddenly out of nowhere I heard a scream. It was right behind a tree. Thinking that a child might have climbed up trying to hide and fell... When I reached it, I saw a pool of blood. It was the little girl! I panicked. I tried to lift up her lifeless body and screamed for help. Her body was cold... I was crying until she opened her eyes and smiled. "Let's play again, ready or not, here I come!" She gave me a push and I blacked out.

When I woke a few moments later, they asked what happened. As I related it, I saw her picture on the wall with some kids. "She's hurt! You have to find her." The head of the orphanage told me it's impossible as she died while playing hide n seek years ago...

Grandmother
Nossebro, Skaraborg Sweden

I was 20 years old and it was time for me to hit the bed.

I have 3 brothers and all of us at that time had separate bedrooms on the ground floor and my mom and dad had their bedroom on the first floor. My mom had a habit during that period of coming down the stairs and checking all the doors and making sure we were alright.

I remember that night as yesterday.

I was in my bed and just read a Steven King book and was about to sleep. My door was open and I could see all the way to the kitchen.

It was dark and from the kitchen I started to hear some noise, like someone was reading a newspaper. I was surprised as I thought my parents were upstairs and that my brothers were fast asleep. Who will read a newspaper in the dark?

I was still looking at the direction of the kitchen hoping to see my mom or dad. Suddenly I saw a silhouette and I thought it was my mom. I called her in a loud manner. It was 20 meters to the kitchen and wanted to make sure that she will hear me, but no answer. The silhouette started to move slowly to my direction and in my mind, that was my mom.

My brain was full of question marks on why my mom was moving so slowly. But now the silhouette was just outside my bedroom door.

I could not see the face and I asked, "What's the matter mom?" I did not get any answer and instead the silhouette moved into the laundry room. I was thinking that mom probably wanted to check the patio doors to the garden.

I waited for a while and I thought, what the heck is mom doing in there for so long.

I got out of the bed to check on my mom. To my big surprise... the patio doors were open. I was in shock, it was a cold winter and a lot of snow. But the thing that shocked me most was no footsteps in the snow.

I ran upstairs to wake my dad up and to my even bigger surprise: both mom and dad were fast asleep.

I did wake them up and told them about what happened and of course they thought I had a bad dream. After a few minutes we had a call from my uncle in Pakistan.

My grandmother had passed away.

The Souls of Dead Babies
Adelaide, South Australia

When you see children's hand painting, you might say to yourself, "How cute," or, "Look at those tiny hands." When I see it, I start to shiver and get goose bumps...

There is a place called Semaphore Beach and near there is a fairly large building that is somewhat like a mansion, which is now surrounded by houses. Now restored to new, you couldn't tell that the building used to be an old, burnt, abandoned maternity hospital.

In 1998, I had a fun night with some friends and decided

to extend the night by cruising driving around. We reached Semaphore with the intentions of getting a thrill from an old Victorian style building.

When we arrived, my mates and I had already hit the ground running. The land there was not developed as it is now, and the only thing on the slight hillside was the building. I remember it was quite dark and cold, you could only see the silhouette of the mansion, and it was fenced off all around like something you would see in a haunted house movie. The windows and most of the doors were boarded shut, which made the place looked creepier.

A couple of the girls who were with us chickened out and decided to stay in the car. However, as the boys and I got closer it started getting windier and much colder... you could hear some of the planks of wood banging against each other.

I started to get paranoid and then images of babies crying as they were being torched alive, a nurse continuing to pour petrol oil(?) or whatever they'd call it in the early 1900's... The story was that a nurse suffering from depression had become unstable and set the place on fire leaving many poor innocent baby souls to perish in the flames. True or not, I'll update this later with some research on the history of the building.

Back to 1998, it started raining heavily. We were not deterred and continued climbing the high fence, where one of the boys was already trying find an opening for entrance. As I was still rattling on the fence, we suddenly heard horrifying loud screams coming from the car.

We ran back to the car thinking that the girls had been assaulted. The screams continued and as we were almost back to the car we saw the driver's door open by itself, which made the car inside lights turn on. We were still around 15 metres away from the vehicle when we were able to see the 2 girls holding each other tight and one pointing and scream at us. Me mates and I looked around and there was nothing to be seen, but their cries told us something was seriously wrong.

As we got closer we had realized that the girls weren't pointing at us and it was clear that they were randomly pointing at the front window screen of the car and there it was...

It was raining, it was windy, it was cold; we looked at the window screen and saw small baby handprints all over the window and all over the car.

Surely this was some sort of a prank. But why were the girls crying? Why were they trying to wipe the window down? I got to the car and tried to wipe the front window screen from the outside, but the small babies' hand imprints reappeared a second after. It was as if dozens of babies were laying their hands on the car and blowing their breath to the window making the hand print marks... Even the rain would not remove the hand markings. "Let's get the **** out of here"!

We sped away from the location, and from the inside of the car the baby hand imprint marks were more obvious. But as we got further away the handprints diminished as if they were letting go of us. But they didn't let us go right away.

The story still haunts me till this day and I still shiver as I did when I was writing this.

Demon Dad
Greer, South Carolina USA

I'm sixteen now, but this happened in Greer, South Carolina, in the year of 1999. I was only six years old.

One night I was in the living room playing with my dog when I remembered I left my backpack in the truck. My mom was in the kitchen, next to the door that went into the garage. I told her that I was going to the garage to get my backpack. I went into the garage shutting the door behind me.

That night was cold and very dark so I was already scared to be by myself. I kept my eyes on the truck since I was too afraid to look at the garage door, because our garage door had windows. I went into the truck and grabbed my backpack. As I did I began to get really worried and more scared than I was when I came into the garage. I jumped out of the truck and began rushing to the door to get inside.

As I was about to grab the doorknob I heard three knocks at the garage window. It scared me so bad I jumped and turned facing the garage window. Looking in the garage window was my dad. He was wearing really dark sunglasses, which is really weird to be wearing at night but

I didn't think about that at the moment. I was relieved to see it was he, but I remained where I was. He didn't smile or speak. Then he began to point. I looked around to see what he was pointing at, but I couldn't figure it out.

"What are you pointing at Daddy?" I asked. No response. He pointed again, remaining serious. I kept looking around and pointed to the garage button. "The button?" I asked. He nodded and motioned for me to push the button. Something inside me told me not to do it.

Dad wasn't acting like he normally does when he sees me after coming home from a long two weeks of work. He always smiles and gives me a big hug and kisses me and tells me how much he missed me when he comes home. Also he always calls to let us know when he's on his way home. I shook my head. He motioned for me to push the button again. I shook my head again.

He lowered his hand out of sight, and just stared angrily at me. The fear I felt began to intensify even more. When he lifted his hand back up there were big long claws. He scratched the window with them. I wanted to scream but the fear I felt kept me silent and I ran inside slamming the door behind me.

I sat on the couch pale and shaky. I remember sitting there terrified and slowly swaying back and forth. My mother noticed something was wrong. She came up to me and asked "What's wrong Vanessa?" I let out a bloodcurdling scream and my mom dropped was what in hand and came to me. She asked what was wrong again. She said that my response was "The devil's scaring me!" but

I remember saying "Daddy's scaring me!" I told her what he wanted me to do and what he did when he got mad. She went into the garage to find nothing there. I felt as if she didn't believe me, but she called my dad to tell him what happened. He was in Houston, Texas, exactly 424 miles east of Midland. She passed the phone to me and Dad told me not to be scared. He said to pray and Jesus would protect me.

The next day my mom went outside to investigate the garage. There on the garage window were three long claw marks. When my dad got home she showed them to him. All that came to his mind was that it was a demon.

But how could something look exactly like my Dad? Also, why was he not speaking and wearing sunglasses? Why would it do that to me? I've been searching for answers for ten years and still haven't found any. If you have any answers I'd love to know.

Poltergeist In The House
Tbilisi, South of Europe Georgia

My family used to have a house that was very old itself, but very well renovated. I was born in that house. I hated that place since I can remember.

I was 8 years old when I first encountered something that I can't explain. But believe me, I get goose bumps when I talk about that.

My mom left me alone for 20 minutes while she went to our neighbor's house. I was watching tv when I heard a very loud noise coming from my mom's bedroom. It sounded like huge crystal vase was dropped on the floor and crashed in pieces. I could not move, I was frozen in the sofa until my mom came. Then when she went in her bedroom I followed her there to see what it was, but there was nothing there.

A few days later my dad, my sister and I were watching tv while my mother was in the kitchen doing something. Suddenly she came to us and asked, "Who was in the kitchen and what did you want?" We looked at each other and said that we had spent the last hour here, but she insisted that she saw someone passing behind her.

Since then we heard a lot of stories from our guests who would come to visit us and spent the night in the house. They heard footsteps at night and they claimed that someone was touching the doorknobs and trying to open them.

When I was there, believe it or not, I always felt someone's presence.

The Pale Man
Norrviken, Stockholm Sweden

My husband and I were walking to the gas station down the road from his grandmother's home as she had run out of milk and needed a liter to begin making dinner. There is one particular house that is closed up and the gate locked. It has always piqued our interest as it once belonged to a family of morticians, and the business was run out of the home. Now it lays empty with old abandoned cars standing all around it.

On this particular day it was kind of chilly, and very cloudy. It was spring and so the typical spring rains had already begun. As we passed the house there was a man standing behind the fence and a blue bag sitting in front of the gate. He seemed to be whispering something, but we could not hear him. He leaned against the fence, and stood there. He was thin and very pale. But did not have an opaque look to him. Just very grey. We walked past and were chilled to the bone by the time we had passed. The chill subsided and we became very warm again.

We picked up the milk and made our way back. When we reached the house the chill had gone, and so was the pale man. His bag or the bag was gone, and there were no footprints and no print where the bag had lane. It seemed rather strange as the walkway from the entrance of the gate was sand and would clearly show prints if someone had been walking there. And the bag would have left clear marks as well.

Since then no one has been spotted there again, and according to land managers the house has stood empty for many years.

No Eyes!
Tonga

This is another experience my sister had while she was holidaying in Tonga.

Not long after their arrival, my sister and her husband went out to the small village bar with some of her husband's brothers. They had a few drinks and enjoyed themselves for a while, then decided to go home, which was about a 15-minute walk from the bar.

My sister was walking with my brother in law a bit ahead of her husband who was walking a few meters behind laughing and joking with another brother. They were coming up to a cemetery and it's Tongan custom to respect the dead and be quiet as you walk by. My sister and brother in law stopped talking as they passed but she could hear her husband still chuckling behind her. No one was walking in front of her and as she turned to look at her husband then turned back to face the front again a man was standing a few meters ahead of her with his head down. She thought it was strange as no one was there only a few seconds before. Warily, she passed him and as she did he said, "Excuse me do you have a lighter?" and she said sure and he looked up and he had no eyes- just black sockets where they should have been. She and her brother in law ran off, with her yelling out to her husband. They reached home before him and when they did her husband said they didn't see any man and had no idea why her and his brother ran off the way they did!

To this day my sister is adamant about what she saw. I've heard her tell it so many times and her story never changes, and I believe her. Her husband's family, most of whom have lived there their entire lives have had experiences, and it's just common knowledge that there are a lot of things that happen there of that nature.

No Face!
Tugucialpa, Honduras

This story happened in Honduras. My mom told me this story, it is also her story. Here it is, hope you enjoy.

She was 10 years old at the time, and she was at her house with her mom, sister, and two brothers. There was a thunderstorm and her power went out. Her mom told her to go to this little shop by her house to get candles. She grabbed an umbrella and stuck on her shoes.

She stepped outside and shut the door behind her. When she opened her umbrella she felt something staring at her. She looked up and saw a man standing there, he was dressed in all black. He started to walk closer to her. She could hear his footsteps in her ear. She tried to scream for her mom but she couldn't.

The man stopped walking, but she could still hear his footsteps. She finally caught her breath to yell for her mom. Her mom came running out! She asked what happened. And she said, "Some man was standing there and he was dressed in black."

Her mom checked the area and she found no one! The next day when their power came back on, her mom called the police. The cops searched everywhere! At her house they have a tall gate because they'd had problems with robbers. The police said it was impossible for anyone to climb the gate.

They kept searching but found no trace of the man. My mom swears this is all true! After that she had a fever for two weeks. She has never seen the guy since that night and she still has no idea who or what he was. Also, the man NEVER showed her his face.

Is She Dead? Am I Crazy?
Glasgow, United Kingdom Scotland

For weeks there was this woman appearing to me when I closed my eyes, even just to blink. Her face, as pretty as it was, really haunted me as I didn't know who she was and why she kept appearing to me. She then stopped appearing for a while but then I had a dream, I really don't like talking about this dream as it really upsets me, but I'd like to share it here now.

The dream started off in a house. It was empty, but when I got upstairs to the bathroom, the same woman that had been appearing to me was being held underwater naked by a man. It was like I wasn't there but I just witnessed a murder! The dream then cut to me at a funeral holding the murderer's arm. Then like some sort of voice-over I hear, "Her name was Anne and she was drowned by her husband who got away with it." Then I turned to the side and she was standing there repeating one thing over and over, "Demons are sharp." I just kept looking at her and did nothing.

When I woke from this dream I felt so sick, I'd never dreamt like that before and it wasn't nice, it made me sad. I went straight to Google to see if I could find anything, because I truly believe this dream happened. I had nothing to go on though so it was useless.

The dream never left my head, still haunts me to this day. Now a few weeks after this dream, a woman called my house phone asking to speak to Maz, that's my nickname. Mum passed the phone to me and the woman sounded so scared and was rushing her words "Maz, Maz, can I speak to Maz!" I told her she was speaking to Maz and she hung up.

I told my mum what happened and didn't think it was right so she decided to phone her back but a man answered and denied that a woman had just called here and then hung up.

It made me mad because I don't like liars and I couldn't help think about my dream. I took the phone and I called back, the man answered again and I asked him why the woman had called, he replied, "No woman called, maybe the wrong number was dialed," and he hung up. The wrong number wasn't dialed because the lady asked to speak to me and she called me by my nickname. I left it because obviously the man was not helping at all.

Now since then I feel someone with me at all times, I've

183

never saw her face again but I remember it clearly. I think it's her I feel, but I don't know for sure, all this confuses me and seems to movie-like to be true but it had happened and I don't know why it happened to me.

Does anyone have any ideas what this could all mean? As I am never going to give up until I know.

I Love You Darling
Rougemont, Vaud Switzerland

Many stories in this app are about how ghosts want to hurt you. Well I have a story that will change your mind.

My friend's father died in a plane crash in Milan when she was three years old. After this happened she became very timid and when she started school she found it very hard to make friends. After a while her confidence came back and she was fine again.

I once went to her house and she asked me a question that made me want to cry. She asked me, "Do you think daddy still listens to me and loves me?" I said to her that he will always love you no matter where he is, but then I said something very wrong. I regret saying it today. I said and his ghost will always be with you. As soon as I finished my sentence she turned pale and screamed, "I never want to see my daddy again!" When she said that everything fell off the shelves and broke.

After that my friend refused to look at me let alone talk to me.

Until one day she came up to me and she said, "I saw him I really saw him, and I was so scared. I really do never want to see him again, why did he come to me?"

I replied, "Think what it's like to be in the same room as someone and talking to them but they can't hear you, you want to tell them how much you love them but they don't understand."

After I said that to my friend, every night "her father" would sit on the end of her bed and talk to her.

And whenever my friend would be falling asleep she would hear: "I love you darling" and felt a cold kiss on her forehead. May he rest in peace.

The Garden Patio

Geelong, Victoria Australia

This story is one that was told by my late Grandad, made believable by events that happened years after death.

My Grandad was old and infirm and couldn't really look after himself. My parents eventually got him a house closer to them in the suburbs so they could keep an eye on him, do his shopping and so on. It was more convenient for me too, when I think back I didn't visit him enough, but did manage to visit him more after he moved to this new place. He was a nice old guy, my Grandad.

One night, we were sitting talking, just the two of us. We were in conversation about something when he stopped talking and stared at the patio doors. I asked what was wrong. He said nothing, but asked me to lock his doors and to close his curtains. I did what he asked me to do and told him he went a bit weird for a few seconds.

He then told me that a woman keeps staring at him through the patio doors. I laughed and said, "Yeah right Grandad, what are you talking about?" The gooseflesh crawled all over my body. He told me that at nighttime, a woman, very pale in complexion and wearing white, stares at him through the doors. She just looks directly him. But she is always gone by the time he gets to the door (took him a while).

According to him it wasn't every night, only a couple nights a week at most, and only at night when it was dark. He didn't have an explanation for the woman at his window. He said it was happening almost every week since he had moved in.

In all the time my grandad lived in that house, no one else saw the woman that he saw. He used to say, "My ghostly friend visited me last night!" Used to get me goose fleshy every time. My parents thought he was losing it. It's funny because I always had this feeling that all his marbles were still there and that he was really seeing something.

My grandad died, God rest his soul. My parents put the house on the housing market to sell and it sold, no problem at all.

About 8 years later, a headline captured my gaze in my local newspaper... "Body Remains Found".

I made inquiries about the exact location of these remains. My parents had never believed the old man, but I managed to find out several weeks later that the remains were below my grandad's patio, on the other side of those doors. The remains were over 100 years old, but an exact date was impossible. To this day the identity of the remains has not been solved, although it was a woman. No unsolved murders or missing persons could link to this person below the patio.

Neither myself, nor my parents have told anyone else about my grandad's ghostly sightings. I sit and think about it at times. Why didn't she wait until my grandad reached the door, she could've told him how she came to be there. She will have told him by now no doubt! When I get too spooked out, I stop thinking about it and pretend my grandad had lost it completely.

I know he hadn't though.

Nightmarish Nights
Melbourne, Victoria Australia

This story gives me shivers just thinking of where to start. I'm literally covered in goose bumps as I mentally travel back to the events.

It's quite simple. It was the night that brought them. Not

just darkness, because you can find darkness in a closet or a dark room at any time of the day. No, this only happened at night. Going back, I think the first time it happened I was ten years old. I suffered from an acute form of insomnia. So I was frequently knocking on mum and dads' door, asking if I can "hop in". Most of the time mum got out of bed, made me a warm drink and tried to settle me in my own bed. But on this one occasion she was too tired, so I crawled in beside her. In mere moments her breathing slowed and her light snores told me she was asleep again.

I lay there, eyes open. Slowly the dark shadows of the room turned into solid forms as my eyes adjusted to the darkness. I could make out the tv, the curtains and the dressing table. I distinctly remember looking up at the ceiling fan and counting one, two, three blades. I lay staring up at where the fourth blade should have been. But it was completely blocked out by darkness. A shadow caused by something in the room maybe. I remember staring intently, physically forcing my eyes to focus. Willing them to act telescopically if only just this once.

Then, almost magically my eyes focused on where that final blade should have been. I froze in abject horror. Absolutely transfixed by the man leaning over me. He was staring straight into the face of my mum. His breathing was ragged and labored. I will never forget the noise. Almost as though he had some lung condition. The nature channel talks about snakes with venom that causes paralysis, making the devouring of their prey easier. Fear was the venom in my veins that night, assisting whatever it was to do as it pleased.

In my peripheral vision I saw movement. I was certain another one of these people were in the room. This one had just bent down to stare into the face of my dad. Then as if they knew I was aware of them, they both turned to stare at me - exactly at the same time. I squeezed my eyes shut, as though doing so would erase the images burnt into my retinas. I may have lay there for hours before i fell asleep, but the next thing i remember was waking up to mum coughing and moaning in the bathroom. Dad seemed very concerned and sent me to make my own breakfast. Afterwards I told dad about my experience and it was deemed that I had a nightmare. Being young and seeking reassurance from an elder, I agreed and felt better.

I forgot about the experience for five years or so. I was now 15 at the time and was still having issues with sleeping. I also remember that I was in pain. My chest and abdomen were terribly sore. The doctor said it was most likely caused by either the way that I slept or some heavy lifting. I couldn't remember lifting anything heavy. This night I lay in bed and stared at the ceiling. Sometimes I would try to see how long I could keep my eyes open. The logic behind it was, if I tired my eyes out then I'd be able to sleep. I succeeded in tiring my eyes and lay there seeking sleep. I let my mind wander but still couldn't sleep. I opened my eyes.

Complete blackness greeted me. I rubbed my eyes and blinked repeatedly but it was still completely black. There was no light peering in from the closed curtains, nor any light from under my door. It was then that the breathing started. Labored breaths. Phlegmy and sick sounding. Just as I realized what was happening, its face came into focus.

It was so close that I could smell its rancid breath. I built up the courage to scream and opened my mouth to do so. But just at that very moment I felt icy hands thrust into my chest and stomach. Awfully cold hands were ripping something inside me apart. The pain was tremendous. I remember punching the walls trying to hit the light switch. The pain and cold was so intense that I was punching because I couldn't unfold my fingers from a fist. All the while I was screaming in my mind. These were screams that haunt me till today. Screams of sheer desperation.

Then suddenly the lights turned on. Mum must have heard the banging. She took one look at me and the room and burst into tears. My left fist was bloodied and the wall had several fist sized holes in it. My blood smeared the walls, but that wasn't what stole her attention. Covering my entire torso was a massive blue, yellow and purple bruise. It looked as though I had been hit by a truck. Mum stood there shaking and crying. She cradled me in her arms and we both sobbed.

Amidst her hushed sobbing I heard her whisper, "No, not my baby as well."

I was taken to the hospital and left overnight for observation. My room was situated on the fifth floor. My hand was bandaged and I was given some sleeping tablets. Mum slept in a chair next to me and got the nurses to keep our lights on. Now that I look back, the nurses were treating my mum and dad rudely. In hindsight, they probably thought my parents had done this to me. The way mum was acting, you'd have thought the same. She was constantly apologizing and reassuring me that it won't happen again.

Mum kissed me on the forehead and wished me good night. Then whispered ever so softly, "You're safe now, Mumma will look after you".

That was the last memory I have of my mum.

I woke up to rain slamming against my face. A vicious wind was blowing from somewhere, making an eerie high-pitched noise. I was shocked to find myself still in the hospital bed. The chair mum was sleeping in was upturned and the blankets were scattered over the room. Fragments of glass littered the floor. I looked around the room and noticed the rain was coming in from a broken window. Shreds of fabric were stuck on the shards of glass.

I stood up and walked slowly to the window, stepping carefully around the glass and pools of water. I looked down and saw blue and red strobes flashing. Police and ambulance vehicles. A sheet of canvas had been placed over something in the centre of the scene. It was then that it all fell together.

"Mum..." I whimpered.

It was all too much. I leaned out the broken window holding on to the window frame with my bandaged hand. The wet wind slapped me in the face and half pulled me out. I took another step forward. This time stepping on glass that stabbed through my bare feet. I didn't care anymore. I let go of the window frame and closed my eyes.

Screams reached my ears, followed by roars of hysteria. Then something powerful lifted me up. Pulling me away from the window. I found myself seated on the bed and embraced by my dad. His rhythmic sobbing jolted my body and I began to cry too.

I am now 25 years old. I have not been visited by those evil things since that fateful night. I don't know what happened to my mum or what she did. But I truly believe she did what she did to protect me. I love you mum.

The Rose
Melbourne, Victoria Australia

I never met my grandmother and from all accounts I wasn't missing much. She was described as a selfish woman whose four children were of the lowest priority in her life. As a result my mum and grandmother were estranged and lived in different states; Nan in New South Wales and mum and us in Victoria.

One Sunday afternoon I went and sat in the lounge room while my mum laid on the couch with her eyes closed, listening to classical music. After a short while I noticed that tears where welling in her eyes. I asked if she was ok and she assured me all was fine it was just the music that was bringing the tears. Although I found it unusual I accepted what she said but continued to watch her face. She looked in grief as her silent tears slowly continued. To me the tears just didn't seem appropriate to the music, but what would I know, I was a kid.

After about 20 minutes the phone rang and my mum

answered it. Mum's conversation with the person on the other end of the line was subdued, not like mum at all who was a loud, almost animated person. I listed as she asked questions of the caller like "when?" and "how?", then she hung up the phone and laid back on the couch with her eyes closed.

The whole atmosphere was strange and I was freaking out a bit. I asked mum who was on the phone. She just said, "No-one you know," and left it at that. I continued to watch her lying there with her eyes closed and soon tears were streaming down her face but she didn't make a sound, just got up and left the room.

I was dumbfounded.

That night I woke suddenly from a sound sleep. It was the early hours of the morning and the house was dark and silent. From under the covers I peered out at my bedroom doorway. Standing in the doorway was the silhouette of a woman. The figure almost filled the entrance and she was standing with one hand on her hip. I sleepily blinked a few times in case I was seeing things but each time the figure of the woman became clearer. She was a large older woman in a dress the showed her bulges and her grey hair was short around her plump face. She just stood there silently watching me.

I pulled my head under the covers in fright and told myself that what I was seeing wasn't really there. After a moment I had to check again to reassure myself but when I poked my head back out from under the covers the old woman was still standing there!

I bolted upright in bed with my eyes fixed on her and I wanted to scream but I couldn't muster a sound, just felt frozen in fear. The old woman dropped her hand from her hip and took a step into the room towards me. I instantly panicked, which broke me out of my stupor, and I leapt straight out of bed. Feeling trapped in my small room I desperately needed to escape and having no other option but the door I ran straight for it and in the process straight through the old woman.

Rushing hysterically into my parents' room I managed to wake everyone in the house. Terrified, I told my mum about the woman in my room as she desperately tried calm me. I was in such a state I wouldn't go back in my room so my dad made up a bed for me in the lounge room.

Feeling a bit calmer I got under the blankets on the couch and my mum sat down beside me. Putting a necklace with a charm around my neck she said, "You don't need to be scared. The was your nana that you saw. That phone call I got today was from Danny telling me that my mum, your nana, had died today and I think she just wanted to come and meet you before she went for good."

"That was why you were crying?" I asked.

"Yes, but I told her that she can't stay because she frightened you. I'm sure she didn't mean to," she said.

"But mum, you were crying before the phone rang," I said suspiciously. "That's because she had already come to visit me to apologize." "Apologize for what?" I asked.

"That's not important anymore. But I think that because she hadn't met any of you kids... I didn't think to tell her... well I just wasn't thinking. But she will leave you alone now I promise."

Even with the reassurance from mum I was still too scared to sleep in my own room for days after that. Each night I would sleep on the couch and each night I would dream the same dream. It was of a window and on the other side of the window was a rose bush with a single apricot colored rose blowing in the wind against the glass. The thorn of the rose would scratch at the glass so there was nothing but a continuing Click-Click-Click sound until I woke up.

Now at the same time every year I dream this same dream.

Tom
Melbourne, Victoria Australia

My house was built back in the 1940's and we are the second family to live there. Along the back hallways there are pictures painted by the previous owners of various things, suns, trees etc.

When I was between the age of 6 and 14 I would awaken in the night to an old man named Tom, sitting at the end of my bed, who would tell me stories of his family and mostly about his daughter Joan.

He would tell me of his passing away in my bedroom, that the pictures in the yard were painted by Joan, about his career on the police force, and that he meant no harm to my family.

Every time Tom came to visit me I would vividly remember our conversation and his stories, but always assumed that I had dreamt it as my grandmother's name was Joan Stedby and he said that their surname was Sted. Eventually the visits stopped and I had forgotten about my dreams of Tom.

When I was 16 I was called into the careers office of my school. Sitting with the careers lady, she was going over my forms when she noticed my address and said she used to live on my street but couldn't recall what number. She went on to introduce herself to me telling me her name was Joan.

When I heard her say her name I got this cold chill down my back and for some reason I blurted that she used to live in my home. I went on to tell her of a man named Tom telling me of his daughter.

I decided to stop when I saw the expression on Joan's face. She was looking at me blankly as though I was insane.

I waited quietly for a moment. She then told me her father's name was Tom, but that I was too young to have met him as he had died in the early 70's, nearly 20 years before I was born.

I told her how I would see him in the night and described the paintings he told me about and that the surname was

Sted. At this point Joan burst into tears as she continued to listen to me repeat toms stories and describe my house to her.

I still live in the house and occasionally I hear Tom wandering around at night. I only saw Tom once again after meeting his daughter, when he came and thanked me for passing on his love to her.

Joan has stayed in contact with me and has been to visit my house, even stayed while we were on holidays so she too could have visits from her father.

The Lady In White
Rio, Victoria Trinidad

When I was younger my aunt told my sister and I the story of the Lady in White. The myth was that she haunted the forest behind the village. My grandmother had seen her. Long black flowing hair, white dress, my gran said she seemed to be floating. Gran did not see her face as she was moving away from her. It was said that she was harmless to women but merciless to men. I laughed at the thought of this story, for little did I know my brother and I would encounter her.

During the summer I was watching my siblings while my dad worked. My mother had moved to America, so I was in charge when he was at work. I was 15, my sister 13 and my brother was 10. It was about 8 a.m. I told my brother to brush his teeth and come have breakfast. My sister was asleep.

Instead of brushing his teeth he went into the back yard. Beyond the yard were the woods. As I could see him through the glass sliding door I let him play a little. I could see that he had two pieces of twigs in his hand but I wasn't sure what he was doing with them.

I could see him stop what he was doing and look in the direction of the woods. Moments later he let out a high pitched scream and bolted toward the house. Hearing him scream, I ran out the house after him. I managed to get ahold of him when he had almost gotten to the house. I grabbed his hand and asked him what's wrong. He pointed behind me, back to the woods. All he kept saying was "She's calling me." I looked but saw nothing. He kept pulling trying to run. Again I looked back to the woods. I could hear sounds as if something was coming toward us. After a few moments she started to manifest. I could see her. She was floating, hands outstretched, her face horrible and disfigured. I couldn't believe it but she was saying my brother's name.

Just then I remembered the story my aunt had told. Instead of running I held my ground. I began screaming at her. I remember saying that she could not have my brother. She smiled a wicked smile and I could see her teeth were razor sharp and pointed. She seemed to fade in and out of form. When she was almost upon us she focused on something I was wearing around my neck: my gran's necklace with a small talisman on it. She screamed, looking at me. I remember seeing her retreat into the forest. I turned and looked at my brother in complete disbelief.

We lived there for 3 more years. My brother never went into the yard without me. When I was 18, I moved out and took my brother and sister with me.

My First Ghost
Rio Claro, Victoria Trinidad

During my early childhood my family spent a lot of time moving around. In the beginning we stayed with my grandparents. I loved living there. The village was small and everybody knew everyone. My grandparents' house was small, flat and woodened. It had three rooms and a large sun room at the front. We stayed in the middle room.

At this point in my life, being about 5 years old I had no idea what ghosts were. So to say I was making this up would be a far reach. My first experience happened in our room while my family slept. The room had two beds that were separated. Most times I would sleep next to dad. My mom, little sister and brother slept in the other bed.

We had just gone to bed. It was raining and there was a lot of lightning. I loved it. Hearing the rain hit the galvanized roof was absolutely beautiful. I don't know what time it was, but I heard a noise coming from where my mother was sleeping. It had startled me a bit. I strained my eyes in the dark but couldn't see much. Again it was there, a growl, I thought maybe the dog had somehow gotten inside.

My dad was sleeping on his side, his back turned to me. I raised up and rested my cheeks on his shoulder. My eyes adjusted to the dim light coming from the next room. At first I couldn't believe what I was seeing. A woman laying under my mother's bed. Suddenly she seemed to be floating. My eyes, they couldn't understand. She was just floating there. Suddenly the lightning flashed and I saw her clearly. She was looking at me! Floating out from under the bed. I didn't know why but I somehow thought I was dreaming, but I wasn't she was there and this was happening and she was coming out from beneath the bed after seeing me.

I slid back down my dad's shoulder and pushed myself almost under his other shoulder. I never screamed or said a word as she walked into my cousin's room next to us, followed by his scream. And not even after the slamming of the front door as she exited the house. I was sweating and scared but never said a word. It was my first encounter with a ghost but certainly not my last.

My Grandmother's House
San Pedro, Victoria Trinidad

When I was 13 my dad moved my sister, brother and I to my grandmother's house. I had always hated that house. It was very eerie. Even as a child I noticed that things were not right there. As much as I hated to admit it my grandma hated that house too, until she died.

Many strange things happened over the years, but my first sighting there happened just after my grandma's funeral.

Volume 1 Ghost Stories from Around the World

The layout of the house is pretty simple. Four rooms on the right, a small porch to the front with a sliding door entrance into the large living room and the kitchen right after. The bathroom and the toilet were the last room on the right, after the kitchen. A couple nights after the funeral, my uncle, mom, brother, sister and I were in the second room talking about stuff. I wanted to go to pee so bad but was scared to go by myself. I asked my sister and we headed off since she wanted to go too.

I let her go first since there was only one toilet. As we walked into the bathroom area we went past the shower. The curtain was only halfway pulled and I could see nothing was on the other side. As my sister finished I go in and I tell her to wait for me. I finish and walk out a second later.

My sister is not in the walkway, but I see someone standing behind the shower curtain that is still only half way pulled. So I'm waiting. I am talking to her but she's not answering me. Suddenly I smell something coming from the kitchen. It smells like the perfume they used on my grandma on the day of her funeral. I'm a little scared and I ask my sister, what's taking so long? Still no answer. I can see the shadow behind the curtain. Frustrated I walked up and pulled it aside. There was no one there.

Suddenly the smell of the perfume got gets stronger and I ran back to the room. My sister was there on the bed playing with my little brother. I asked her why she left me? She looked at me, puzzled and said, because you said I could go back to the room. I never told her to leave me and that was my first of many experiences at that house.

I don't know if it was my grandma or not, but I certainly did not want to find out.

The End of Volume 1

Joe Kwon's True Ghost Stories

Ghost Stories from Around the World

Volume 1 Ghost Stories from Around the World

Have you seen a ghost?

Submit your encounters at
www.kwonapps.com/publishing/haunted/

Joe Kwon, Inc.

Joe Kwon's True Ghost Stories. Copyright © 2010 by Joe Kwon, Inc. All rights reserved. Published and distributed worldwide from the United States of America. No part of this book may be used or reproduced in any manner whatsoever without written permission except in the case of brief quotations embodied in critical articles or reviews. For information, address Joe Kwon, Inc, 3 North Lafayette, Marshall, Missouri 65340.

ISBN-10 0-9828659-7-X, ISBN-13 9780982865972

Joe Kwon's True Ghost Stories